Under Pressure
Permission Changes Everything

John D. Martin

"Forward" By Roberta Natale

Copyright 2010 by John D. Martin

All rights reserved. No part of this work covered by the copyrights hereon may be reproduced or used in any form or by any means-graphic, electronic or mechanical, including photocopying, recording, taping or information storage and retrieval systems-without the prior written permission of the publisher, or, in case of photocopying or other reprographic copying, a license from Access Copyright, the Canadian Copyright Licensing Agency.

ISBN 978-0-9866196-0-1

www.changeitbooks.com

Contents

"Forward"/ vii
Preface / ix
This I Claim / xiii
Introduction / xv

Part One: The Red Letters

Help / 3
Our Stuff / 9
The Words / 15
Us and Them / 35
Be Careful / 39
Button Your Collar / 43
You're Kidding Me! / 53
We Kill Our Kids / 67
Get Off Me / 79

Part Two: Permission

Now What? / 85
Something Completely New / 89
Self Care / 95
The Big P / 101
How It Feels / 109
When I Was a Child / 113
Yesterday / 121
Relationships / 129
Listen / 139
The List / 145
Tomorrow / 153

For
Constance and Zechariah
who never stop providing for me

and

For my dear friends, Linda who has seen me through this never wavering always with me and Roberta whose courage is inspirational and future so full of possibilities.

Yesterday brings us
to where we are, it does not have to take us to where we
are going.

Live like everyone is watching all the time.

The most important page of all
Very special thanks to new friends and old.

For you Cheryl Kossen, without your editing patience and ability I would have looked foolish.

For you Victor Kozak, without your skill and kindness this would still be pages on the floor.

For you Dave Cannon, who makes sure I think, dot every i and cross every t.

For you Adnan Abosh, who skillfully brought us to the world.

For you Heidi Winter, your experience and enthusiasm help me remember why.

For you Barbara Durette who has helped me make so much come to life.

"Forward"

I have known John Martin for several years. When he was working on **Under Pressure...Permission Changes Everything**, he gave me a portion of it to read. That particular section of the book contained a character that was based on me. Of course I was flattered and intrigued to read it, however, after reading I felt angry, misunderstood and disappointed. When John asked me what I thought, I told him that "he didn't know me at all; I wasn't the person he made me out to be." He encouraged me to read the entire book, but for months I refused.

What I didn't know, was in that moment, my life was changed forever. As much as I tried to shrug off the experience as though it didn't matter, I found myself thinking about the book and my feelings around it every day. I began paying attention to my reactions in life's daily challenges so that I would not fulfill the prophecy of this "character." I convinced myself that I was not her and in doing that I was catapulted into self awareness. When John gave me the entire book to read, it took me a long time to convince myself to pick it up. When I finally did I became unhinged.

Under Pressure asks, "Do I have the courage and the confidence to resist the pressures around me and pursue the things that I feel are important?" The answer to that has always been very clear to me, I have responsibilities in life. I owe it to everyone around me to fulfill those roles to the best of my ability, even if it consumes me. It's what I "should" be doing because it's the "right" thing. Considering the possibilities outside of my obligations was unimaginable.

Under Pressure...Permission Changes Everything will wake you up and teach you how to stop walking through life blindly. Through real life examples you will learn how to identify what is holding you back so that you can reach your true potential.

The purpose of ***Under Pressure*** is to provoke thought, reconsider the status quo and endeavor to find a new approach.

The message in this book will be delivered to those who are listening. The message may come to you as a revelation or a process. Either way it will strip you down and compel you to consider the possibilities and challenge you to do things differently. Under Pressure may take you on a bumpy ride, but the destination can be life changing. My life is shifting into a higher consciousness and ***Under Pressure*** has been my ticket for this journey.

Roberta Natale

Preface

The work before you has been constructed in two parts. The first part is a matter of fact, simple look at some of the reasons that contribute to who we are and why we act and re-act the way we do.

In an effort to make it all real and easy to relate to ***Under Pressure...Permission Changes Everything***, uses dozens of anecdotes, real stories from real people that I have encountered over my life time. Listen and see if they don't make you smile and wince. They are all, you and I.

Part one is called The Red Letters or to be more precise six words that have too often come to define and determine us, six words that can and often have enormous control and influence over our lives and our sense of being.

The Red Letters show how we have been "turned on", controlled and dictated to by the most powerful institutions and organizations in our society. They have cleverly used the words should and shouldn't, right and wrong and good and bad to manipulate us and make sure that desired ends are met. They have done that so skillfully, that we have made these words and their power our own.

We follow prescriptions, often having no idea why, and we are led to places that do not fulfill us. These are places that speak of mediocrity, conformity, fitting in and being accepted. The consequences of not fitting in are simply too great to ignore.

It would be safe to say that the first half of the book is a tool to gain reference and perspective. It's meant to be a bit like finding a map and saying "so that's where I am" and then spending some time with that map and saying "so that's how I got here".

So many people ask "why". The Red Letters offer some possible answers.

The second half of the book Permission, is somewhat unusual. Continuing the map analogy, it says "ok, now that I know where I am and how I got here, how do I get out of here?" More importantly, "how do I get myself to a place that might be more authentic, more acceptable to me, more honest and more hopeful?"

My life experience has taught me that permission is a wonderful tool and gift. Once we understand its power and ability relative to our lives, others and the world at large, there is no telling how many new, currently unimaginable possibilities might be easily within our grasp. From here, we build on "The Facts" if you will, of the first half. Now we are no longer information gathering. Now we are going to try something new, something fresh and something potentially life changing.

***Under Pressure...Permission Changes Everything*, is a very simple piece of work and certainly a "true story."**

Come and see how permission works, where it can take us and what a wonderful place that can be. Let me show you how to undo the power of The Red Letters and how, maybe for the first time, your entire perspective and your whole life might finally be yours, full of new, happy and self fulfilled. Come and see possibilities never before imagined and how to do so many things completely new.

This I Claim

All of the people that you will read about in the coming pages are very real. I have changed their names and sometimes their gender because I do not want to embarrass anyone.

I either know the people that I use as examples in my life today, or I have dug into my memory and accessed those and their stories from the past.

The people are real, the stories are real and the message that you are about to read is very real.

When I started to write I had only two requirements. I wanted what I wrote to make sense and to mean something.

I do so hope that it makes sense and means something to you.

j m

Introduction

At 5am on a very cool late March day, long before daylight, the solitary figure of a small thin woman with brilliant red hair sat on my front step.

Passing by inside, I staggered and drew back. I could see through the glass door a person where no person was expected to be.

As my eyes drew focus, my head slowly followed, I knew this shape. I took a deep breath, I knew the story.

No words had been spoken. She did not know I was there, that she was not alone. Yet already somehow we were united, together.

We sat, held hands, came close, moved away, shivered and felt.

In time she spoke.

"I need something, but I have no idea what. My soul aches, feels so heavy. It's hard to breathe. I am a good girl lost."

Her search, her spot, those words and that encounter helped to bring what follows.

Part One

The Red Letters

Help

Robert drives the same road each day. He passes the same shops and parks and likely most of the same people, and he wonders how and why. At least he wonders why on a good day, a day of reminiscence and maybe melancholy. Most days though he is simply angry at his life, his lot and his pit.

He seeks me out on occasion simply to talk or I guess to spew.

"How did I get here, how come I am so fed up, so angry, what happened to my life?

I had dreams and plans and then, Jesus, I'm just so angry I can barely function.

I can't stand my job, I'm behind on my financial commitments and my marriage is in shambles.

I mean it's not a total mess, but most of the time we only cope, you know, two people trying to survive, trying to make sense, hoping to do better. Two people, who wonder, at least to ourselves, why are we here, what's in the future and at times why we bothered to marry at all.

I don't say it, she doesn't say it but I know we both think these things. We both get lost and wonder why and how to do it better, or even if better is possible.

In fact, most of my life has no resemblance to what I thought it would be. My children drive me crazy and at times I don't even want to be a parent. I feel horrible, even feeling this is terrible for me, saying it is beyond comprehension.

Don't get me wrong, I love my kids but it's somehow more than I imagined it would be.

I mean, I wonder, is this what I signed up for? Is it going to get better and can we find a different way?

Tell me that thing I like to hear. Tell me that thing that makes it better, that actually helps for a few minutes, that thing that makes it stop and gives me hope.

Tell me that thing that makes me smile and laugh. That thing that you say, that I believe when it comes out of your mouth, that thing that you seem to actually believe. Tell me!"

Robert is a friend of mine, and he, like others that I know and have known, share a similar problem. They are in a place that makes little sense, a place unplanned and unknown. A place that came together by circumstance or worse, a place made by others.

"Fret not my friend so much of what you worry about, so much that drives you to despair is fixable.

You have the ability and the opportunity to do things differently, to change course, to give that stuff up and to make huge and significant changes.

Robert my friend, you have permission to do things differently."

Each time it's the same. He looks at me in disbelief, peaceful, mouth-open disbelief, and, for an instant feels the power of possibilities and feels the hope of something new and different.

"I love the way that sounds, and sometimes I can keep the hope of something new and different for a day or two.

But you know how it goes. Life gets in the way and in an hour or a day I'm back, back in my stuff and those words seem ridiculous, untouchable and almost a mockery to my life.

Maybe if you would write them down, put them on paper, maybe then I could reach for them when things seem out of control, when I am lost or frightened or completely hopeless.

Just write them down so that I can remember and while you're at it, write down that other stuff. You know, all the stories and the hope and the how to and the permission and how it all seems to work and how while I sit here in this artificial, "it's not really my life" place, it all makes perfect sense.

Write it all down, damn it, so that I can hold it and hear it and feel it."

Ashna didn't believe it when she heard it. She was utterly incredulous, beside herself, yet she never said a word.

For ten minutes we sat together in a small group, nothing more than lunch-time chatter. There was talk about something and nothing. Today, Ashna dominated; she needed sympathy, empathy, maybe just an ear. Ashna, told us about her evening, a night gone wrong.

"It's the same thing every time we get together.

I have these two friends, you know, guy friends. We've known each other since high school and we get together every couple of weeks, see a movie, have dinner, drinks, whatever.

Every time it's the same thing. They have too much to drink. They act like fools, say stupid things, sometimes mean and hurtful things, usually inappropriate sexual things and it bothers me. They don't respect me and my feelings. They don't care about how I feel and they couldn't care less about what it's like for me to be with a couple of fools.

And every time it's the same thing the next day. One of them or sometimes even both will call." *"Sorry Ashna. I guess we had too much to drink. I guess we said some things that might have hurt you. Sorry Ashna. You know it's the booze. We'll do better next time."*

"I guess I can forgive them. I mean, they are my friends. We've known each other for fifteen years, maybe more.

That's what friends do isn't it, support each other and understand?"

And the room nods and listens and respects Ashna's pain, and the room gets it.

Of course, Ashna needs to forgive and be patient. Of course, Ashna ought to understand. That's what friends do, isn't it? That's what the room thinks. She is justified and cared for. She is vindicated and supported. The room understands her pain and her predicament.

Is this all Ashna can hope for, a group of work buddies, lunch time "friends" nodding and excusing Ashna's inability and her friends poor behavior?

"You don't have to keep the same friends.

There is no rule that says you have to keep the same friends forever. Why bother with them and why not be without them?

Are you compelled to be here? Is there something that says a friend once is a friend forever?

Lose them, get some new friends. Find someone who respects you, cares for you and treats you decently.

And if that's not possible then be by yourself. It's got to be better than this.

Do it differently. Of course, you can forgive and be understanding, but enough is enough. You can still forgive or even understand these people without having to be abused by them, week after week and year after year."

Ashna looks at me with disbelief, utter disbelief. Such a thing is spoken in a foreign language. Such a thing has never occurred to her. She is not only caught off guard but she is absolutely shocked at the notion. How is such a thing possible? How can steps like this be taken? She simply stares blankly.

This is my life, her face says. This is what I have, my lot. How on earth can such action and freedom be possible?

"Ashna, pretty much anything is possible. Certainly your life and its betterment, your happiness and choices that bring happiness closer, are very possible.

Ashna, imagine the freedom of not participating in the same mess, the same ugly mess over and over again."

She simply stares blankly, hoping to decipher this new language. The silence is clear, lunch is over.

Our Stuff

We get our stuff, our sense of what we ought to be and ought to do from a number of places.

We get wound up and turned on, motivated and directed from voices within that inevitably come from voices without.

This is how we become who and what we are and this is what establishes our frame, our sense of reality and most importantly the code or codes that we live by.

For the sake of discussion let's call this our environment or our socialization. Some would argue that this stuff is innate, intrinsic and somehow part of our soul. They would argue that as people we know just what we are "supposed to do", we just have to scratch away at our surface to figure it out. I'm not sure. I am sure that pretty much anything is open for discussion.

There was a time that I believed that surely we could find a common thread, a common group of principles or beliefs that could keep us together. They would allow us to agree at least on the really important things, the basics or fundamentals of being human on the same planet.

You know, don't kill, don't cause others harm. Don't be malicious. Don't consider yourself first, or at least not first all of the time. Consider other people's needs and wants. Be decent, be kind, and considerate and respect other people. The list goes on, the bottom line, thank you Rodney King… "Can't we all just get along?"

I believed that we all somehow saw things pretty much the same when it came to the really critical issues of humanity. I needed to believe that as long as a common system of basic human decency and understanding was possible, then I was very much able to have a real sense of hope for human kind.

I needed to maintain the fantasy that when push came to shove the very vast majority of people, regardless of culture or family roots or religious orientation, would dig down deep and pull the best of themselves out of their very being. They would hear that voice that unites all people and choose to do and be the decent thing, the caring thing, the "I really do give a damn" thing. And that somehow, that thing, would, at its very core be similar enough for everyone, or at least everyone who wasn't clinically disturbed or mad, that caring, decent behavior would somehow rise up and prevail.

Viktor once told me of being at the scene of a terrible accident on the highway.

"It was a total mess. There were at least fifteen cars involved and two huge trucks. Many people were hurt. We learned later that three people died right there on the road.

It was in the middle of a blinding snowstorm. We were going the other way and we were somehow able to see it all happening. Cars and trucks just kept running into each other.

The amazing thing was that people were running into the mess, into the wreckage to try and help those involved.

It was incredible, even though you couldn't see properly, even though there was clearly the sense that the accident was not over and danger was imminent, people left the safety of their cars on the other side of the road or behind the mess and ran, seemingly with no thought, into the fire, the screaming, smashing metal and glass.

I remember feeling so proud to be a part of that. I remember feeling proud to be a person.

I don't think anyone was saving or trying to save or help a friend or a family member but people responded bravely and with determination. They were going to help no matter what the cost. It was beautiful."

Viktor's experience is what I needed to believe people were made of in all critical situations. When the chips are down, when our backs are to the wall, decency and a concern for others will somehow prevail.

Sadly, my life experience and the experience of so many others that I have learned about, shows me absolutely that that wish is simply that, a hope.

I wanted to believe that somehow, at least when it came to the really important things, the important "stuff" of life, there would be a "common agreement" that would under all circumstances keep us all nodding our heads. I needed to buy into the dream that we all "got it", that when push came to shove the very vast majority of people would somehow be able to come together on the basics of life, recognize a thread that unites, at least on the very most essential concerns of being human.

I am no longer sure. So much seems fluid, relative and uncertain. The truths that one person or one group hold are often foreign or even ridiculous to others. Some of these basics are chalked up to social and cultural differences. In this country we eat with utensils, in that with our hands. In this place we speak face to face, here we do not make eye contact. In that land we marry our relatives, in this we wouldn't dare, couldn't. It would land us "in ridicule" or maybe even in jail. I shake hands, you bow. She hugs and kisses on the cheek, he stands at attention. The list of we do it this way and you do it that way is endless and often humorous, however, sometimes it's not funny at all.

Daryl is an African man that I knew years ago. He once told me a most astounding thing.

"In the land that I come from, many people are dying from AIDS. It is widely taught, at least on the streets and in the community that the best and only way to cure oneself from this horrible disease is to find a virgin and have sex with her.

Many people in my country believe that the "cleanliness" of the virgin will cure the illness.

12

Of course, the only way to really guarantee that you have found yourself a true virgin is to find a very young child and be sexual with her.

Because of this belief and the need that this belief has created many parents who are in need of food for themselves or their families are selling their very young, female children to those infected with AIDS. This accomplishes two things. The starving family has a little money to survive another day and the child sold as a "cure" is now likely infected as well."

See what I mean?
Daryl's story is certainly extreme and very sad, but it is a shocking example of how what can be tolerated, even accepted in one place, one culture, one group, is beyond belief and absolutely intolerable to another.

These extreme examples are much more common than you might first think. The truth is, there are many examples of human behavior that are considered acceptable or even mainline by one group that are utterly repugnant to others.

Are they wrong in this African place, are we right here? Maybe, but not all cases are so clearly obvious and chances are if asked, many of those in Daryl's land might not have a big problem with "sacrificing" virgins.

On September the 11th 2001, for me one of the most shocking things that I witnessed was not the obvious. Oh, I was beside myself at the horrible and blatant acts of murder perpetrated on civilians. The planes, the explosions, the bodies, the tumbling buildings were all beyond my ability to comprehend. None of these images, though, are what is most left with me today, several years later.

The world really is a global village now and as a result we have the ability almost instantly, to not only witness events live or capture events minutes after the fact, but we can gauge reactions instantly as well.

I remember standing in front of my television, mouth agape, as I watched some in other countries celebrate, what I had seen only minutes earlier as barbarism, murder on a grand scale and acts of hatred beyond human comprehension.

While I was collecting myself and literally pinching my flesh to see if my senses were correct, others celebrated in the streets in huge numbers cheering the death and destruction of others.

A short time later while some parts of the world were cursing and trying to capture a man called Osama, in other parts of the world he was honored and his name given to a record number of males, newly born.

Point made, your reality may be a very long way from mine or from the next person's.

The things one person considers acceptable may be worlds apart from that which is acceptable to others. The least common thing about our common point of view may in fact be its commonality.

The Words

All this got me thinking. There are in my life experience and my culture six words that ought to be re-examined and carefully considered. Six words that are very powerful and potentially harmful. Six words that can manipulate and control, push and pull and have so many of us doing what others have thrust upon us rather than being responsible for who and what we are.

I call them the Red Letters.

When I hear them or read them I laugh, smile or shake my head and think these words are so powerful, so dramatic and so very controlling that when written, ought to appear in red so that everyone who comes in contact with their presence can immediately understand their power and be alerted to their significance.

We all know them, chances are we all use them on a very regular basis and we all, or at least the very vast majority of us, use them as tools, knowingly or not, against others and believe it or not, against ourselves and our own very existence and happiness. These are the Red Letters. They control, harm and keep us from our own growth, development, learning and humanity. In fact, they may be at the core of many of our daily, social and cultural problems. Certainly they speak loudly to Robert, Ashna and those in the places like Daryl comes from.

The Red Letters definitely go in pairs. They are stuck together as if somehow to be given more power. It is very difficult to have one without the other and together they cause manipulation, misery, pain and often destruction of the situation and the individual.

They really ought to teach courses on these six. In the English language and in Western society there are as far as I can tell, no more loaded words, words that carry such clout and such damaging consequences. These are words that tear and define, judge and condemn. They are words that hurt and pigeon-hole, words that ought to be behind glass, words that might require an act of emergency in order to use them. I find it difficult to separate them. They all somehow are one in the same, but for the sake of our consideration I will group them in their natural pairs. Beware of their power; beware of their weight on your very existence.

Should and shouldn't are the first duo. This pair we pull out at a moment's notice or worse, with no thought or notice at all. We have decided that these two S words are worth using whenever we see fit.

You should go to church.
You should cut your hair.
You should go back to school.
You should kiss your father good night.

16

You should eat less food.
You should paint your walls blue.
You should buy that dress it looks good on you.
You should, you should you should....

Of course there is the evil twin.

You shouldn't stay out so late.
You shouldn't see that boy any more.
You shouldn't listen to that kind of music.
You shouldn't wear black; it's not your color.
You shouldn't give so much freedom to your children.
You shouldn't eat so much yellow cheese.
You shouldn't go to that school any more.
You shouldn't, you shouldn't, you shouldn't...

The list is as endless as your imagination or your life experience. The pain that these lovely S words can cause is beyond explanation. I have no doubt that at least with those who speak English (maybe other languages too) that we have all been subject to the pain of the S words. We have all felt the humiliation of others telling us what we should or shouldn't do, how we should or shouldn't live, what we should or shouldn't eat or think or believe or consider or so much more.

Strangely enough, I would go further and say that even though most of us, or I dare say all of us have been on the difficult end of should or shouldn't that we do not hesitate to fling the S words ourselves. We hurl them in the direction of passersby, acquaintances, friends and even family. We toss them with a kind of certainty and superiority, pretty much at anyone or any situation that we choose regardless of the consequences to those who the S words are directed at.

Apparently, we have learned nothing from our own misery. Instead of "turning the other cheek" we simply take the sting of the slap and as quickly as we are hit, turn to our "neighbor" whoever that may be, and slap them in return. Why don't we learn?

Why don't we "get it," pause, consider what the words feel like when they are directed at us and stop the "pass it on" insanity then and there?

Alana is a young lady who lives with her grandmother. Her grandmother is definitely from "the old country" and does not approve of many of the choices that Alana makes.

"I can't do anything without her telling me that I should do this or I shouldn't do that. She "should and shouldn'ts" me on my appearance, my work habits, my choice of friends, my eating habits and my studying. I am so tired of the ridicule and the judgment. It feels like I can't do anything right.

The really strange thing is that my grandmother has made me so should and shouldn't sensitive that I hear it everywhere. I have turned into a should and shouldn't freak. Once my grandmother sensitized me I hear the words everywhere. My friends use them all the time, my teachers, I can't get away from the stuff. How come everybody knows what I should and shouldn't be doing with my life better than me?"

The pain that Alana feels from her grandmother is the pain of should and shouldn't. These words are meant, on their own, to hurt, to cause guilt, to manipulate and to somehow have the recipient feel lost, alone, judged and most importantly anxious, that somehow they have not lived up to expectations. They don't make the grade, they have failed or disappointed. You do not approve and "they had better get it right."

No good can come of these feelings. There can only be a wicked sense of self loathing, personal failure, a lack of self worth and most disturbing of all, an urge to join the crowd.

Should and shouldn't almost on their own, have the awful ability to force the individual out of us, to make us conform, feel small, out of sorts and alone.

Resist the "should and shouldn'ts" that come your way. Resist those who toss them at you and resist the pain that they bring.

If you have the patience, explain to those who "should or shouldn't you" what they are doing, how you feel, or if possible give them a copy of these words. Don't forget that as hurtful and small as these words can make you feel that you too are likely guilty of thrusting them, often without thought, in the direction of others.

Sadly, many use these words as commonly as they might say hello or good bye or report factually on something. The truth is that we "should and shouldn't" each other all the time without much thought at all about what we are doing. We have very little insight and therefore, I suppose very little responsibility.

I ask you then to pause for a moment and feel the weight of the S words. Wait until they are used in your direction and if they have not stung you before, listen carefully. Listen with more than your ears and hear them differently. Feel their pressure, and then try to live life not judging, condemning and deciding for others. You will feel differently and those you encounter will respond in a new way to your concern for them, their freedom and their worth.

David is a man of thirty-one who had such a hard time with his family.

"My sisters are so judgmental. They are never satisfied with me, my choices or my life. For years they told me what I should and shouldn't do. I am the youngest and if I didn't do things the way they thought I ought to then they were relentless.

Basically, if I didn't do things their way then I was wrong or worse, a failure.

I finally got the courage one day to confront them. I told them how their "should and shouldn'ts" made me feel and the strangest thing happened, they heard me.

It wasn't immediate but they began to try.

There is no way that I can explain how my life has changed. The load that I carried, always trying to measure up, to do it their way, anyway but my way, was immense.

I risked and told them what pain they were causing me and how I felt manipulated and they responded. My life feels so different.

Now, if I could only get the rest of the world to 'get it'."

You, like David, have the opportunity every day with those who are important to you to help them so that they in turn can help you. David risked and challenged his sisters. They heard him and responded. As a result, David feels better, more human, and freer.

Life goes on, but differently now. David is beginning to take responsibility for his life and his world. David does things differently and he will make a difference. David does not have to cringe at his sisters' needs and their inability to see him as a person. He has begun to be an individual with all its wondrous shortcomings.

Remember Robert from the beginning? Robert, is this what you meant?

We are just getting started. The Red Letters go on and may even "get better." I will offer the next four in pairs; however, they are so closely connected that I could easily group them together. This next coupling make should and shouldn't look tame. Hold on, the ride is about to get really interesting.

Right and wrong are once more words of distinction.

They are words that have enormous consequences and power and that can cause us to feel a variety of things. As with should and shouldn't we carry them in our sack of tools and we pull them out, usually in sanctimony, attacking anyone who does not meet our pleasure.

He was wrong to act like that.
She was wrong in her decision to marry him.
They were wrong in sending their child to that school.

Finally, they got something right.
It's only right to wear a long dress to an occasion like this.
It's not right to associate with people like that.
That's not right, they aren't right, it's not right.

The list once more is endless and again the judgment, condemnation and accompanying pain is huge. We seem to have decided, often all by ourselves what is right and wrong. We are judge and jury, and more, we are often the executioner too.

We sit with arms crossed, metaphorically or in reality, and decide based on our life experience or our personal code, who and what is right and wrong. We condemn and judge, we point and reject, we take our sanctimony and push it into the lives of others and they feel it, react to it, respond to it and they hurt. They are again manipulated, forced to comply, to fit in, to knuckle under. They had better or else they will certainly feel the wrath of right and wrong.

Worse than that they hide, and they lie and they cower and they so often do whatever it is that they need to do, to get our approval, to get the "right and wrong" monkey off their back.

Fit in.
Be approved and accepted.

Above all else, keep the group, the team, the club, the "village" happy with you.

Again we don't get it. Every time that we clobber someone or some situation with the almighty right or wrong we are doomed to be beaten ourselves by the very same fist. I remember reading somewhere that the measure that we give will be the measure that we get…hmm.

I'll judge you, then you judge me, then I'll judge you, then you judge me, then…

That's wrong.
You're wrong.
They are wrong.

Finally, someone is right to tell them off.
I've never been so right.
It's not the right hair cut for her.
It's only right to wear white between May and September.

The list, the suffering, the harsh judgment of right and wrong is satisfying.

We love it, revel in it and enjoy the superiority and the ability to condemn and decide.

Come over here. Let me have a close look at you and your stuff. Let me pull it all apart and see what I can decide is right and wrong. Moreover, let me see what tune I am going to play for you to dance to.

Make no mistake, once you are in their sights or they in yours, there will be a lot of dancing, or a lot of hell to be suffered.

Hold on we will get to that.

"Small communities" and groups are especially good places for right and wrong to thrive and flourish. Do not get caught being an individual in a small community or as a member of a group. Do not exert your uniqueness if you are a member of a group, a club or a team.

No, no we don't like that kind of thing "around here."

We are not comfortable with "that kind of behavior."

We would rather not see you "acting like that."

It's usually quiet and whispered but if you continue or don't get the message then the pressure is likely to mount.

Julia was a very popular girl in high school. She had a number of friends, did well scholastically, was very pretty and always had the attention of the boys. Julia was tall, shapely, witty, bright and terribly unhappy. At 17 years old she tried to tell her closest friend that she was different, she didn't fit, that she was gay. Her friend was beside herself, maybe relieved, some thought later.

Not only did her friend tell her she was wrong but she decided then and there to pressure Julia into seeing the error of her "choice." Not only did Julia's friend condemn her, but she wrote to Julia's family exposing" the secret." The family was incensed. No child of ours was going to be "like this."

"You are wrong and we are embarrassed." Julia tried to cover her shame and say it was all a lie, just a misunderstanding.

Within three months she had been completely ostracized.

She drank and slept. She was drunk, depressed or completely lost in her "wrongness." She tried to hide.

Within six months she had moved from her small town to the big city but she left with a crushed spirit and a broken heart. She left not being accepted, loved, cared for and mostly, not being "right."

Julia was dead before nineteen. They say she died of a drug overdose.

No, it was a huge terminal case of malicious small "townness," small "groupness."

Or if you like, a classic case of "can't you get it right, you are so wrong."

Did they learn from Julia? Did her mess teach them anything? I would be very surprised.

In fact, Julia gone is just one more person who was wrong that no longer needed their attention.

I suppose there are times when things are clearly right and wrong but the really interesting thing is that for as many people asked, the definition of right and wrong may change. Of course there are the central issues where hopefully there is the some kind of agreement.

It is right to be kind, right to be truthful, right to be generous and right to be faithful. Without doubt, for every right, there is a wrong. It is wrong to lie, wrong to cheat, wrong to steal and wrong to be violent.

These seem clear to me, even enshrined somewhere in human consciences. Think so? The next and final set of red letters can easily ruin any idea of beginning to feel good, any sense of agreement and coming together.

They are the heavy hitters. They do not bend or bow in anyway. They are steadfast and absolutely ugly in every sense, and they round out the set of three to perfection.

If you have managed to get through should and shouldn't and right and wrong be prepared, anything that you may have left of your spirit and your sense of fairness, justice, decency and humanity is about to be shaken.

Allow me to bring you face to face with the most potent, nasty "Red Letters" of all.

Good and bad are the ultimate Red Letters.

Should and shouldn't have a subtle quality to them. The S words are merely a suggestion. They imply that you might reconsider that maybe you are on an incorrect path.

There ought to be a change and you might still be able to fix the place where you have made a mistake or are misguided.

Right and wrong, are certainly more forceful. They bring the weight of certainty with them. There can be no doubt. You have erred and you need to change your ways, immediately. In fact, change your ways or else.

Or else, you might end up like Julia, cast out, ridiculed, rejected or worse; you might end up "just like Julia".

But good and bad have it on all of them, because good and bad conjure up the absolute and I think even the divine. These babies invoke the "will of God" and now you are really in trouble. Now, even the almighty disapproves of you, your actions and your situation.

There is no telling how much damage has been done over the years in the name of good and bad. One cannot imagine how many lives have been altered, disturbed or completely destroyed.

If we look even for an instant at history, the results are shocking and catastrophic. Entire civilizations destroyed in the name of good and bad. Wars have been waged based on "you and yours are bad and we therefore are good". "Our way is good and God-like and yours is bad and therefore evil."

Even today, many conflicts exist, at this very moment, because of the power of good and bad. Groups and full societies are certain of the absolute guarantee of their way and their system and of course of the lack of worth and credibility of any other way.

Religions and governments are both guilty of this horrible act of hatred towards others. Simply translated it breaks down to we and our way of doing and thinking is correct or good, while you and your way is incorrect or bad.

Then it's on. The righteous group has to go further than simply insulting their neighbors. No, in these cases an insult will not do. Now they must go further and turn their disapproval into action. Before you know it, there is another ethnic conflict, a holy war or a racial mess between two groups and it is always and only, based on the massive power of good and bad.

These situations speak to the world in turmoil and conflict. They offer up pictures, either of our world history or our very day that ought to cause us shame and humiliation. Unfortunately, quite the opposite seems to be the case. The righteous, the holders of "the good," continue to pound on the unholy in their midst and with a sense of certainty and false pride, they go about their work of hatred with such a vengeance that no amount of reason or compassion can call them off.

They, after all, have God on their side and therefore they are "in the right." They represent good and goodness itself and nothing must get in their way.

This history, or geopolitical lesson, true as it may be, seems a long way from so many of our lives. My house is not on fire. No one is pointing a gun or even a finger at me. My street is safe to walk down. My life or belief system is not threatened in any way that I am aware of.

Of course I can read and I am aware of some of the atrocities happening elsewhere. I get the conflicts and the hatred in the world, but by and large, I get all of this stuff from the comfort of my safe, secure place.

This whole good and bad thing doesn't really affect my daily life. So it would seem.

"I live here and I am safe, it really doesn't involve me."

Good and bad are not solely the domain of governments and religions. They are not the exclusive property of fanatical groups that seek to wage war on other groups, and certainly are not only about those who have a "holy cause" and want to alter the world.

There are many among us, most I believe, who have no interest in changing the world or bringing a new "God" to your neighborhood but who are so full of fear, contempt and loathing for anything "different", or unusual or not "cut from the same cloth" that they conspire, all on their own, to damage anything "out of the ordinary".

No, I am not providing you with a conspiracy theory and I don't believe that we are in imminent danger from some lurking force.

I do, however, believe that when should and shouldn't, right and wrong get going, when they gain strength and power, that good and bad are only around the corner and that for many in our world, the only real way that they can go through life is to categorize and classify.

Richard is a man I have known most of my life. For more years than I can remember he has been an ardent supporter of his religious organization. He attends services every week and of course, he is there front and centre on important occasions. I saw him recently and he seemed forlorn.

"I can't go anymore. I can't buy in any longer. They are supposed to tell me about the important things in life. The things we can't forget. You know, love and peace, compassion, acceptance and forgiveness.

Things are different now. We have a new clergyman and he seems to have forgotten some of the basics. He is aggressive and I think completely misses the point.

Now he speaks about our differences and how we are not supposed to drop our guard. We must be careful not to let "bad" in.

We are to keep pure and good and we are meant to be on guard for the bad and for infiltrates.

What the hell is going on? You know what the really disturbing thing is? I am pretty well the only one who seems to have a problem.

I have been going to this place for more years than I can count and I know most of the people who worship there, but they have changed.

I seem to be the only person with a problem.

Recently I spoke with three people about the change, the intolerance, the push on words like good and bad and the mindset that goes along with it all.

It's the strangest thing. Of the people I spoke to, three good solid people, people I thought I knew, not one of them had a problem with the change. Now they teach and preach separation and segregation.

The mentality is completely different. I can't be there any longer. I am devastated. This group and this community is a place that I believed in.

The change is scary and I need to get away from it. Imagine, we are good and right and they, they meaning everyone who isn't us, are wrong and bad and we need to "watch" and keep them away."

Richard's sense that things were moving in a difficult, if not the wrong (oops), direction seems to be the scary truth. The really frightening thing is that no one else seemed to care about the new course and focus of his religious community. This, unfortunately, is how things seem to go. For some reason, it is easier to move to the lowest common denominator than to move to a higher, more honorable spot.

Whipping people into frenzy, to do horrible, nasty, selfish or even unspeakable things seems to have a great deal of historical precedent.

Finding examples of large groups being incited to care about or concern themselves with others is much less common.

Ironically, even places when there is a claim to be truly interested in good, just and decent causes, places like religious groups, governments and schools, often find themselves at the centre of evil-doing.

The pronouncement of good and bad ought to be avoided whenever possible. Yet even in our most basic teaching, even with the very young and most impressionable, we load up the stick with the heaviest possible weight on the end and plunder children with the most powerful words at our disposal.

No Jimmy that's bad.
You're a bad boy Jason.
Good girls don't do things like that.
Go to your room and don't come out until you have learned to be good.
Josh, wait until your father gets home and I tell him how bad you have been today.
Nehil, bad girls like you, don't deserve dinner.

The words that we need to be the most careful with are words that we do not hesitate to pour over our children. I am guessing that if they make an impression on adults, good and bad, also leave a child full of things that hurt and scar, things that may take a life time or longer to purge.

Children hear very well, they get the message perfectly. Listen sometime to young children playing together or even speaking to a toy, a doll or a stuffed animal. They mimic what they have heard and they freely pull out good and bad to show approval and disapproval. The stuffed animals never had a chance, good and bad are heaped on them and by the end of the play session, and doll therapy is clearly in order.

Us and Them

Occasionally, something is so important to the whole that it gets it's very own spot.

This next bit is just such a thing.

All of the Red Letters come from one important place, a place of the human condition and a place to be reckoned with.

I am certain that if evil or awful goes unchallenged that it gains strength and permission to thrive and grow, take root and fester until all of the "apples" have been ruined by the one.

Under this metaphor, before you know it, the norm will be ugly, damaged and dangerous.

Any time that we can manage to fall under the spell of "us and them" then we are at the mercy of should and shouldn't, right and wrong and certainly good and bad.

Division is essential to the Red Letters. There is always a left and a right, always a "this way" or "that" and always the acceptable and the not so acceptable.

A number of years ago I had the opportunity to spend time with a young woman from the West Indies. Her name was Jenel. She was delightful, and in only a few weeks taught me a great deal about her culture and about the people that she called "her people".

One day her brother came to pick her up from work. He came into the place where we were and stood in the corner. Jenel had gone out of the room for a moment and so in an effort to be social and decent I went to greet him, welcome him and assure him that his sister would return in a moment or two.

I approached him with my hand out. As I came close, he put his hand in his pocket, glared at me, made an angry step in my direction and said "come closer and I will hurt you".

I was in shock. I had done nothing to provoke this. In fact, I only wanted to be friendly and make him welcome.

I backed off and before any incident occurred Jenel returned, got the picture very quickly, took her brother by the hand and left for the evening.

The next day when she came to work, Jenel told me that her brothers, all seven of them, hated white people. In fact, she went on and said that it really wasn't safe for a white person to be around them. Normally, when such a thing happened, as it had with me, there would very likely be violence.

I couldn't believe what I was hearing. This was beyond anything that I had ever heard, let alone felt.

The next day Jenel quit work. She called me one day later and said that her brothers did not know that she worked with a white person and that they insisted she quit.

In hindsight, I am sure that Jenel quit to protect me.

On the day between the altercation and her leaving, Jenel explained to me that her brothers hated white people for all of the pain and suffering that the white people had caused black people over the years.

"But Jenel" I recall saying, "it makes no sense. I am not the enemy. Why punish me for the crimes of others?

Why stay angry forever?
Anger only leads to more anger. Nothing is ever healed or solved this way."

"You don't understand. For them, it's simply a matter of "us and them" and if you're not one of us then you are one of them and "them" is not wanted any time, in any way."

This is the fuel of the Red Letters. This is the key and the crux and this cannot be stressed enough. "Us and them" is what should and shouldn't, right and wrong and good and bad are made of. They feed on this.

Every should has a shouldn't. Every right has a wrong and every good has a bad and as long as we can divide, as long as we can separate, then the Red Letters and their power will grow, damage, and in the end prevail.

We are not "us and them," we are not black and white, male and female, we are simply a species looking to exist, and we all share a common space. That space can be one of turmoil, anger and hatred or it can have other options. First, however, the Red Letters must be exposed for what they are. We must see the power they have and there must be an understanding that we will paint them red, recognize them, and acknowledge their ability to separate and cause harm.

Most importantly though, we must see the way they make the world and all in it, separate, contradictory and opposed. They make it, "us and them."

Be Careful

If we have any hope at all, any chance whatsoever, of doing things differently then we must first understand exactly what we are dealing with and where the separation and the ability to divide comes from.

I have mentioned the power, the absolute, terrible power of these six demons. Should and shouldn't, right and wrong and certainly good and bad are first and foremost here to divide and separate us.

They centre out the one or the ones who have not lived up to expectations and once exposed for who and what they are, that is wrong, and away from the standard, or worse, different, then there is an expectation.

At first it's usually fairly subtle. The individual or the group, who has decided that you are not quite up to scratch, will let you know that you or your action or point of view, are skewed. You have fallen short and you are off course.

"Come on Jodie, you're not like us anymore. You don't fit in. Your behavior is silly, crazy, wrong. We don't approve, we need you to change and get back to the flock.

You used to be so much fun. We could depend on you. You're not the same any more. What happened to you Jodie, you've changed."

If that doesn't work there might be an intervention.

Again, there are usually hints so that you might get the picture. Maybe you don't get called to participate in group activities. Maybe you are told somehow, in some generally underhanded way, that you have erred or gone astray. Today that might include a text or an e-mail from an unknown source. Or worse, it might even involve a face to face "discussion" from those who "want to be of help to you."

Look, I am not really talking about the differences that occur between groups and individuals on a regular or daily basis. You dye your hair brown and the rest of us are blonde. Who cares? You might even get some credit for "being different," although even here, someone will have a problem. You "brownie," rocked the boat. You altered the status quo and there may be a bit of flack to deal with.

I am not talking about you reading a science book while the rest of us read romance books. Or you driving a foreign car while the rest of us drive domestic cars. These examples are insignificant, however, even in these trivial areas and countless others like them, there will be some resentment. You will be the subject of annoyance, suspicion and even cause for concern, albeit small.

40

Some groups are so unable to cope with any variation, any change at all, that even the blond going brown will cause there to be a casting out.

"Listen Selma, we don't feel comfortable around you as a brunette. We think that you don't fit anymore or worse that you are trying to tell us something. Don't you approve of us anymore?

What's the matter? Aren't we good enough for you?"

Even in the simplest places, there is scrutiny. Be careful, fit in or else. In some groups, some places, not fitting in is the norm. Don't be deceived, the "group of rebels" is as predictable and similar in their thinking as the group of regimented monks who are afforded no freedom or diversity whatsoever.

"Hey, Jimmy, we are all going to get our fifteenth body piercing and beat up a poor person.

What do you mean you're tired of that?

What's up with you, you're a freak. You don't fit in."

You see it never ends. Most of these examples are virtually irrelevant and really pretty silly. The reason I use them is so that we can laugh at ourselves and most importantly begin to see how things, even at this level, operate. Rock the boat at all and be prepared, there will be consequences.

Even groups who pride themselves on being different and unusual are still suspicious if you're not "pulling your weight." "Don't you dare 'not be different.'"

Of course, from here things escalate and get worse until the person or people involved are completely shunned, totally rejected or worse.

You might be surprised to find out where all of this sanctimony, judgment and condemnation come from.

You might be surprised to know that the three main places that have instilled this sense of acceptable and unacceptable in us, are places that many of us have come to trust the most.

It may very well come as a shock to us, that the places that have taught us to be on guard and vigilant to any changes, subtle or otherwise, are places that are responsible for shaping our core. It is very unlikely that many of us or even any of us at all, have been able to escape the influence of these prominent and influential three.

Button Your Collar

Occasionally, we come across a reality that is so difficult to believe or understand that it is hard to take in. Fortunately, we seem to have a built-in protection mechanism that allows us time to digest the reality of the situation. Events that are painful, traumatic or horrible come with a physiological tool that helps us to take in the information at a more acceptable rate of speed.

When my pet dog died a number of years ago I needed time to adjust to that painful reality. Strange as it sounds, I saw him die, yet still I looked for him and truly expected to find him in his usual spots.

Walk-time came and I would reach for the leash.

Feeding- time had me going for the dog food. I can't tell you how many times I reached under the table with a bit of food scraps (I know not the thing to do) expecting to feel his cold nose and his wet chops.

Each time I was saddened at the reality. More importantly, each time I adjusted a little more to the truth of what had happened. It took a significant time for me to really catch on, for me to truly get that he was gone and appreciate that my life would from then on be different.

Fortunately, my psyche allowed me to digest the death of my dog and the changes to my life, slowly. We often do not have the capacity to take things in all at once, so our system filters and allows a bit at a time, so that we can manage the change and the information.

I don't mean to be melodramatic, but when I put together the course, pattern and origin of the Red Letters, when I realized that they have been perpetrated and supported the way that they have, I was stunned and needed that coping mechanism once again.

It was as though someone presented a conspiracy theory to me for the first time and it made great sense. I had to pay attention and I had to adjust my views and my life accordingly.

Many people in the Western world will be able to relate and recall the feeling that they had, when as a child, either by design or by accident, they found out that there was no Santa Claus.

I know on first reading it sounds silly. "Santa, are you kidding. I thought this was a serious book.

What is Santa Claus doing in the middle of it?"

Please bear with me and remember, if it applies to you, how you coped with the "loss" of Santa or how you managed to adjust to the death of your dog or worse the death of someone close to you.

If what I am about to share with you is or has been known to you then I ask for your patience. The fundamental importance of this reality is paramount to our perspective, the way we act, the way we treat others and the things that we think are important.

The Red Letters, should and shouldn't, right and wrong and good and bad have their greatest allies in the three places that we, as members of a culture and a society, any culture and any society, have come to trust the most.

The reason that we hold these words and their meaning so tightly and honor their importance so dearly is because their origins are places that make us who and what we are.

It is virtually impossible to separate the power and depth of these words and their limiting, judging, calculating, conforming, segregating message, from our most trusted life spots.

Once we uncover the roots of the Red Letters, once we accept their birth place, we might and likely will, begin to re-examine many other things as well. My belief and contention is that this re-examination will lead us to some new, exciting and very interesting possibilities.

Hold on, we will get there soon. First, be prepared to find out that there may be things much more disturbing and difficult than facing the loss of something very important to you.

There is really no easy way to say this. No disguise or soft landing to cushion the difficult truth. Should and shouldn't, right and wrong and good and bad have root and are nurtured in our schools.

Indeed the education system that the vast majority of us trust and look to for information, development and truth is a place, one of three, that uphold the smallness, the limiting factors, the segregation, the "us and them" and the judgment of these words and their power. The education system guards them jealously and makes no bones about needing to maintain them and hold them up as values of the highest worth. Jeremy attends a private school. His story is unpleasant.

"We are so full of rules and regulations that it's hard to get to anything else. We wear uniforms, of course, and you should see the list of rules about how to dress.

There are more than five pages devoted to our appearance, the length of skirts for the girls, the length of hair for the boys and the height of the heels on our shoes.

I get it. We wear uniforms so that we are not "competing" with our clothes, that we are not inappropriate or God forbid, that we are not too expressive.

But even if we forget the uniforms and buy into the reasons why, there is still all that other stuff.

We have rules drilled into us.

Boys ought to act like this and girls ought to act like that. This is acceptable and that is not.

All the rules keep us in line, the same old line.

Schools claim to want us to think on our own but really they make it clear that we are meant to do things the way that they have always been done.

You know that "you are the future stuff" is really just another way of saying carry on and be just the same as yesterday.

Protect our way of life and the way we do things.

In our school they keep talking about "all for one and one for all," you know, "you are just like the next guy." The reality is at our school, everybody comes from money and even though they never say it, there is an understanding that we are not at all like the kids in the public school system.

Somehow we are different, maybe even better.

It's never said and I can't put my finger on it, but it is certainly there. You can feel it."

Yesterday's truths and standards are most certainly upheld, supported and presented, one way or another, as tomorrow's answers.

Jeremy has, whether he knows it or not, hit the nail on the head. He understands even if only by the number of rules on dress, that the school he attends holds certain things to be valuable and untouchable. The role of a gentleman, the place of a lady would never be promoted today in my society but it is clearly there, nevertheless.

Imagine a history or sociology class that taught yesterday's mistakes and then, taught ways to make today different. Imagine education promoting change. Consider a system where, not only new scientific discoveries or old history lessons were taught, but rather, new ways to approach the problems, new ways to consider and think.

Yesterday's mistakes are important. We don't want a new generation of leaders who think its okay to invade a neighboring country or it's a good idea to consider genocide or infanticide. Neither do we want to continue to repeat the same old power of the Red Letters.

Schools and the education system in general, are full of rules and regulations. They present the same "stuff", by and large, that our parents and grandparents lived by and who knows how many generations before that. All of the "shoulds and shouldn'ts," "rights and wrongs" and "goods and bads," with few exceptions, are still being supported, and presented as the way to think, relate and act.

Examples beyond Jeremy? No problem.

The global economy doesn't work very well and we have the ability to change it. Imagine redoing the way we balance the world's accounts. Imagine actually taking responsibility for feeding the hungry instead of moaning and wringing our hands over the fact that there are massive numbers of starving.

Imagine if we taught people, while in school, how to truly communicate with each other. What if we taught them how to listen and share their feelings and hear each other, without judgment and segregation and "us and them"?

Have you ever seen the power of a very popular high school student who goes out of his or her way to sit with or pay attention to people who are not particularly popular?

Have you ever seen the massive good that positive peer pressure has? Imagine teaching that, or better, rewarding that.

What if we began seeing that we are somehow "all" related and that we don't want to simply feel sorry for those in places like Africa? We can learn to truly respond to them, so that when someone hands us the "wheel" we know how to drive differently and change the mess.

Imagine a high school credit course on giving a damn?

Or a junior school course on caring for each other and really meaning it.

What about a recognized program on celebrating our differences instead of only our similarities? What about a course where we could actually share our feelings, and got credit? Sorry, I mean a real high school credit for honesty, soul searching and truth telling.

In the Western world, universities are interested in more than students' academic achievements. They are now paying attention to the person's character and how they have participated in, and responded to, the community.

Wow, so the student has to demonstrate, real or otherwise, that they know that they are a part of something bigger than themselves and bigger than their school.

Ridiculous! Why not make it all part of the curriculum? Students could actually be required to show that they understand something about the important things of life, while in the classroom. The system could teach a course or courses on the Red Letters and what they do to us.

They could show that caring and compassion, communication and sharing could be a part of the expected routine. We could show the young how to treat each other and therefore the world differently, and we could commit to change, the same way that we have committed to the history of war or the theory of relativity.

Yes, math, science, history and English are all important, legitimate courses, but surely by now we can stand back and see that these things on their own mean little, if not nothing at all, without a balance and a completely new perspective.

The premise is flawed and the approach has become redundant to the point of being silly.

The education system can and must challenge the activity of the world. To simply examine the ways of yesterday and the breakthroughs of today without getting the bigger picture is to advance nothing but the past, and the past loves the Red Letters and what they do to us.

The past pushes the red letters forward as things to hold onto because the past is seen as worthwhile. You know, the perception, "if it isn't broken, don't fix it".

It is broken beyond any glimmer of repair.

The education system can throw out the "shoulds and shouldn'ts" of the past, examine the mistakes and teach it new.

It can teach "if we learned to respect each other, listen to each other and care for each other's position, then conflict will lessen."

It can teach us that right and wrong are so often relative and changing, that we need to pay attention to the few, the very few grains of "truth" that can honestly unite us and toss the rest into the pile of "suspicious material."

Education can show us at a very young age, and continue to teach us, that good and bad are words created in order to gain some kind of result, and that we might consider them carefully before we hit each other over the head with them.

Unfortunately, the education system is the least of our problems when it comes to advocating the power and the influence of the Red Letters. Of the three places that give the six most dangerous words in the English language credibility and real force, the education system is most definitely, the "weak sister."

The next two may cause you to re-evaluate your very foundation.

You're Kidding Me!

The power of my six least favorite words cannot be overstated. In English and in pretty much every other language, I suspect, should and shouldn't, right and wrong and good and bad, have enormous clout.

The damage that we can inflict on each other by using any of these six is beyond words.

It is really important to understand why they have so much power, why they are potentially so lethal.

The answer is simple, and scary, all at once. They seek to control us, manipulate us and keep us in line.

They want us doing as we should, keeping things right and always being good. It even rhymes!

It is easy enough to see why the education system has bought into the Red Letters. Education is, after all, in the business, at least in part, of controlling large groups of people. Education must control us on the most basic level of human activity because education has the responsibility of seeing to it that large groups of people, usually young people, ought to act in a way that will keep them doing what they must do.

It's simple. While in school, you must behave yourself and act in a certain way. You must not be a threat to the safety of others, don't rock the boat physically. Certain "out of line," or "out of control" behavior is not acceptable.

I have no problem with any of this. Children and young people together in large groups must abide by certain clear, simple rules so that someone does not get hurt. Aggressive physical behavior, for instance, is unacceptable. We do not want someone harmed. Bullying must not ever be tolerated. It sends the wrong message and does not protect the weak. These are all good things and speak well to crowd control and basic rules of conduct when a bunch of people, especially children or young people, get together.

Beyond these basics, however, the education system has fallen short and failed miserably.

We need to be creating open minds, minds that question where we have come from and minds that seek real alternatives. Turning the square a little, so that it now appears as a diamond, is not a real alternative.

Education can take some of the responsibility for the mindless sheep mentality that is prominent in the world of human behavior today. Whatever you do don't think on your own. Don't be an individual. Don't set new standards, don't do things radically different. Of course, if you spoke to an educator they would tell you that they compel the youth of today to grow and experiment. They would be offended at these "sheep comments" claiming rather that they encourage young minds to set new standards and "see things differently." The curriculum presented in mainline North American education would suggest strongly that the way we did it yesterday is certainly the way to do it today. The opportunities for education to "do it differently" are immense.

Teach us how to understand each other. Teach us how to cope with our feelings. Teach us how to listen and care and respect. Teach us how to fix the problems that an inequitable world has created, and mostly teach us how to act and respond. Teach us how to relate and listen, without the threat of the words I so dearly hate.

Drag should and shouldn't, right and wrong and good and bad out into the light and let us look at them. Let us understand what they have done to us and what they continue to do to us as individuals and as societies and then let us put them in their place, not stripped and worthless, but understood and void of the ability to destroy and even kill. This is what education could do for us.

This is why, in its current form, education is a miserable failure, teaching only about yesterday, offering little new about tomorrow and protecting the status quo. Whether it knows it or not, the education system, propagates the truths of yesterday and says clearly that real human growth and understanding, true human development and change, are unimportant and irrelevant.

Until education helps us to examine our core and our roots and helps us to see worthwhile alternatives, little will ever change

This is massive opportunity lost.

Let me give you a very small tangible example. In the school system, that I am most familiar with, there is a relatively new mandatory course that helps the high school students learn how to better cope with the working world that they will soon be entering. They learn how to write a letter to a perspective employer, how to write a resume and how to respond in an interview, among other things. All of these tools are worthwhile and have value, however, this is what the education system, where I live, thinks is the way to prepare teenagers for the world.

Imagine a course on understanding the others in your class. Imagine understanding how to listen, without judgment, or, for that matter, how to listen at all.

Imagine a course where students tell stories about what the six words have done to them and how to cope with the expectations of others.

Imagine wanting to send young people into the world with a set of tools that we now only reserve for those who have explored or studied psychology or philosophy or certain types of medicine.

Imagine a world where we knew how to hear, how to listen, how to care and how to help. For me, this can only mean that education is complicit. They either do not want a healthier world where we might really learn to do things diffcrently or they have no idea how to do things differently, or there is some unknown force that keeps them doing things as they have "always been done."

That thought is disturbing and brings me to the second cause for the power of the Red Letters.

Education is often a tool of something much more powerful and certainly much more influential. Education of course gets its cues from a much greater place, possibly two greater places. Education is simply a puppet of something with real teeth that truly has a strong vested interest in control and having us comply.

Historically, in every society that I am aware of, education has taken its lead and gotten its direction from the force and the power of religion.

Religion, unlike education, has no need to be subtle and no need to claim to be doing something else. Religion makes it clear from the start that it has our best interests at heart and religion has much more. It has the absolute, certain word of God as its backbone. God is religion's witness and its right to manipulate, control and judge.

I don't know about all religions, but I do know a bit about two or three, and a fair amount about one or two others and they all make the same claim. They all know what's best for you and I, and they all claim the right to make that and its consequences, abundantly clear.

Religion does a better job of not having a hidden agenda, but make no mistake, while they are busy helping you live a "better life" or get "closer to God" or find the way to "peace or heaven", they are also absolutely interested in controlling you, how you think, what you do and, in the end, especially how you feel.

Some religions are, without doubt, much more aggressive than others. Some are much more forceful and certain that they, and only they, have the answers that all people crave. I find it interesting that often the "more religious," at least in the traditional sense that a person becomes, the less freedom they have and the more the religion dictates to them.

The very religious have most things already determined for them. Their life style is set. They know exactly how to act and even how to re-act in most, if not all situations. In many cases, there is such a strict set of rules and regulations that little or no thinking or choice is required at all.

It would seem, then, that the closer that one seeks to move towards God and deeper into religion, the fewer options that are available. Your dress is often chosen or at least suggested. Your diet may be a foregone conclusion and certainly your daily activity has already been set according to standards established many years or, in many cases, many centuries ago.

In some faiths who you can communicate with and what you are permitted to communicate about, are set. Furthermore, who you can and cannot associate with is determined. And marriage, if you are so inclined, if in fact inclination has anything to do with it, is virtually predetermined. Strict moral rules exist and in many cases any and all social, ethical and certainly theological questions have already been answered, clearly by people who somehow had all the answers.

Wow! I guess if I had a problem with the limiting nature and opportunities of education, religion must drive me to distraction. Yes indeed.

I am not a religious expert, but I get it. It all involves submission, adherence and a commitment to following a certain set of suppositions, set down and decided by those more qualified or more indoctrinated.

I figure, if you want to sign up and it's good for you, then suit yourself. Go ahead, be an adult, make your informed choice and carry on. At least that's what I would like to think initially.

The more that I think about it, the more religion frustrates me and drives me wild. I get that religion is at the forefront of those words that I loathe and therefore at the forefront of things like separation, manipulation, segregation, and maybe most importantly, us and them. Without doubt religion has it all figured out, made all the decisions and caused as much human pain and suffering as anything else conceivable.

A number of years ago I knew a man very well who had attended a religious college. He was not a particularly religious person but he attended university and took some courses at a religious part of the school.

This college was one of a number of "religious affiliated" schools that were amalgamated within a secular university and, at anytime, any student was able to "crossover" from the main part of the university in order to take courses at one of these colleges. I can still vividly recall his take on this particular aspect of his post secondary education. He told me that his time at this particular college was wonderful. That many of the professors had fantastic reputations and the courses were, by and large, terrific. He didn't realize until sometime after he had graduated what an influence his time at this particular part of the school had had on him.

"I had, even without my full knowledge, become indoctrinated. Over the years that I studied as an undergraduate, I had taken several courses at the college and by the time I was finished I knew the answers to so many questions. This part of the university made no bones about it. Their point of view represented a particular faith. Certainly, many schools of thought and many possibilities were explored but in the end the point of view presented as "correct or most sound" was in keeping with this particular faith community.

It was wonderful. At first there was such a peace, such calm in me. I had the answers to all the difficult questions of life. I didn't have to struggle or wonder or worry. It was all clear. I simply needed to remember what to do in a given situation. My moral or ethical dilemmas were answered. My "mystery of the universe," metaphysical questions, were answered. And certainly, any "God questions," questions of theology were right in front of me. It was fantastic, if in doubt check "the book."

It was all there as plain as the nose on your face. I mean it was wonderful until a couple of years later when I got my head out of my "academic backside" and began to live in the "world of ambiguities and ambivalences."

I finally left school and had to deal with real people in real situations and very quickly some of the "proven formulas" didn't work so well. Now I was dealing with real people in real situations and the answers from "the book" often made little or no sense. I realized then that religion, or at least this convenient stuff that I had learned, had no interest in us as people with confusing, human problems. It only had an interest in making sure that the prescriptions were followed. Prescriptions set hundreds of years ago by people who had other things in mind. This I figured out was more about fitting the people and the situations to the answers, not finding answers that fit people and their real needs. I was devastated and needed to start all over again."

My friend understood clearly the devastating power of religion and truly why I have such a hard time with the whole thing.

Are we understood through religion? Are we nurtured and cared for as individuals?

Is there a real and genuine interest in helping us lead fuller more rewarding lives?

Do the problems, the real difficult problems, of being human get addressed? Is there an appreciation of our uniqueness, an understanding of us and our lot? Is our situation today and how it might differ from yesterday noticed? Are we given credit for being individuals?

Certainly not!

Religion is not only the propagator of the six hateful words, but it is also very likely their keeper as well.

Surely, should and shouldn't, right and wrong and good and bad are happiest when cared for and protected by religion. These scary words and most religions are on the same page.

Most religions have no problem with decrees and prescriptions. In fact, religion delights and revels in these things.

Religion represents rules and acceptable behavior. It sounds like they took the script right out of the definition of my six friends.

Religion divides and separates us. We are divided first and foremost into huge groups. You are Muslim, you are Jewish, you are Christian you are, you are, you are and you are.

Oh, and you, you appear to be with no group at all. You really have a problem.

You know how it goes.
We are correct.
We have the answers.
We have the truth.

I guess sadly the corollary is also true.
You are lost.
You are wrong.

You are out of luck.
You do not have God.
We have God and you therefore…

Then we divide the groups into sub groups.

You are Roman Catholic and we are Protestant.
You are Sephardic and we are Ashkenazy.
You are Shiite and we are Sunni.
You are orthodox and we do not observe as closely.
I have roots in this tribe or caste and you in that.

It never ends and each time there is division and separation. Each time there is a suggestion or a tone accepting and rejecting, condoning and rebuking.

Religion loves the Red Letters and will protect and defend them to the death. Yes, religion does a lot of things, "to the death."

Religion thrives on the stuff that defines us. It causes us pain and segregation that divides and judges and that causes us to shun our neighbor.

We are called here under these formulas, to cast off the non-believer, to separate ourselves from the other and to gather in a protective angry circle against the world and for the power of the ugly words.

Marie is a woman now in her midlife who was speaking with me about religion recently. She remembered vividly her catechism and the confirmation ceremony that followed. She recalled the excitement when those in her congregation learned that the Bishop himself was coming to attend the service. I watched her face change quickly; however, as the story went from excitement over the special visitor all those years ago to what happened next. Marie recalls that certain children were chosen in advance to receive questions from the honored guest.

"The Bishop would, with the whole faith community present, ask a few children planned questions and the chosen children would of course provide the correct answers.

Marie became visibly angry when she told me that the local priest was quick to tell the specially selected, that they would face punishment if when called upon by the Bishop they got the wrong answer to his question. There was no room for error. Even as a young child only certain answers were considered acceptable. Marie simply shook her head at the story's end. Maybe they could have handled that differently."

Poor Marie got clobbered as a little girl, beaten by all three at once.

You shouldn't make a mistake. You must get it right and you will be bad if you mess this up.

The feelings and needs of the individual are irrelevant. The pain suffered by feelings of exclusion or being ostracized or by not living up to standards is the manna of religion.

They will claim otherwise, but religion loves and needs the Red Letters.

Religion is should and shouldn't, right and wrong and good and bad.

Religion may have been intended to do exactly the opposite but simply look around. The pain of being forced to comply, to not be different and to care less about you and your needs is religion's base.

There is no spot for you and your needs. The Gods do not recognize that.

Religion in many places has evolved into the ultimate place for rules and regulations. They each have a book full of should and shouldn't, right and wrong and good and bad.

I want to be very clear here. I do understand and appreciate that every person who aligns themselves with institutional religion and every religious group or sub group is not guilty of blindness and "closed group thinking." I do not want to throw the baby out with the bath water. I know that there are many good, committed religious people who struggle to make a difference

I am fairly certain that the original intent of most major world religions was not crowd control, however, that is exactly where we are now.

Here are the rules. Memorize them, live by them and for goodness sake don't drop the ball or we will be forced to exclude you, "exorcise" you or maybe even execute you.

The Red Letters and religion are nothing more than opportunity lost.

We Kill Our Kids

The third member of the unholy trinity responsible for fostering and protecting should and shouldn't, right and wrong and good and bad is the most distressing, disturbing spot of all.

On some pragmatic level education and religion have a real vested interest in having us "do as we are told."

They are organizations and institutions that are responsible for large numbers of people and as a result they have a commitment to mass-producing behavior and "truth."

They need to have a required outcome from those who are "plugged in."

At the end of the day, education and religion are both trying desperately to have people "get it."

That commitment requires a number of sacrifices. The individual, their feelings, and inevitably their happiness, become pretty much unimportant.

In fact, anything beyond getting a very large group of people from point A to point B is very difficult. A commitment to a simple direction is really the biggest, if not the only, concern.

I am reminded of the feeling of leaving a stadium after a sporting event. No matter how comfortable your spot was in the arena, once it comes time to move to the exit and outside, the journey is fairly unpleasant and a bit awkward.

There is no doubt, however, that those responsible for moving the crowd, and the engineers and architects who built the facility, knew exactly what had to be done. People are moved in a sea from the interior to the exterior with a kind of herd-like precision. The ride is not especially pleasant but it is clear that you are headed to the door. In fact, you really have no choice. You must move with the crowd or find yourself potentially battered, injured, or even worse.

This is education and religion and this is how they have chosen to handle and process us.

Here is the stream, get in and the current will take you to where you need (oops) where we need you to go. If you are looking for something individual or special, something unique or personally tailored, well, we have lots of words claiming to have things exactly custom fitted, but really, we are all in the same boat.

I think it is a terrible let down and shock when we realize, if we realize, that our schooling and our institutional faith have been handled in such a crass, uncaring way. It can make you wonder what you believed and invested in. It can make you question places that you were told, even convinced, cared for you as a unique person.

The third member of the scheme to sell and protect the power of the Red Letters is much more devastating because now we are not pitted against an institution, some huge uncaring cattle-processing thing. It's no longer the feeling of little you and the huge uncaring, unfeeling "thing". No, now we are face to face with our own families and our very own parents.

Indeed our parents, those most responsible for who and what we are, may be the biggest disappointment, the biggest let-down of all.

There is a link between a child and his or her parents that connects. There is a bond that provides certain assurances and guarantees.

You will look after me and care for me. You will help me and protect me. You will make sure that I am recognized and seen as important.

You will love me and accept the love that I, in turn, offer to you. You will tell me the truth and encourage me to be a truthful person.

You will teach me the things that I need to know and you will help me sort and understand the differences that are difficult to interpret.

You will help me to be the best person that I can be and you will do all you can to see to it that my life has some quality and meaning.

You will care for me and about me at all times and even when I am lost, confused and in pain or despair, you will be there with me and for me. You will understand my

needs and my form. You see my soul, my strengths and weaknesses.
You are my teacher, my guide, my inspiration and my friend. You care about my happiness.

To the best of my knowledge this, along with other similar important things not mentioned here, is the basis of the parent-child agreement. This is never printed out or signed, however, this is the understood bond between parents and their children, maybe even the world over.

This is the foundation on which the parent-child relationship is formed and secured. No, these words are not exchanged at some ceremony, spoken upon the birth of a child or even necessarily taught to a child or a parent as they grow. Nevertheless, they are a given.

For some parent-child relationships these sentiments may only exist in a hope somewhere. Their reality in any form may have, for one reason or another, never been possible. Regardless, they exist in hope.

For other parents and children, these words may have had meaning once but somehow the meaning, the commitment, has slipped, maybe even gone completely.

Still for others the words have an enduring presence and even though living up to all this wonder might be difficult, even impossible at times, both parent and child know that the structure is in place and is unshakeable.

This is why the pain is so great in this corner and this is why the reality is most difficult to swallow here. I can clearly remember being told as a child that police were my friends. That if in doubt or if in trouble, seek out a police person. They will help you, they will take care of you and they are definitely people that you can trust.

I can remember that for years I believed this. I recall feeling safe if a police officer was near and I felt confident that no harm would or could come to me if I was in their presence.

My world and my world view were somewhat shaken when as an older child, maybe a teenager, I learned through reading the news or paying attention to the things around me that my assumptions, and therefore my teaching, was not true.

It was with some difficulty and certainly with a large dose of "I don't like growing up" that I came to see that all police were not necessarily my friends. Certainly, all police were not guaranteed to be people that I wanted to trust automatically.

I use this example because it is very much like this when we see that our parents, our own care givers, who are supposed to, above all else, care about us, our development, and our happiness, cannot or are unable to.

Indeed the very first or last line of defence, (depending on your point of view) between you and the real cold, "We don't give a damn," world is your parents.

Didn't they get the memo, the message?

Didn't they read the book?

They have to know what to do. They have no choice but to tell us the truth, help us first and teach us about life's real problems and the pit falls.

Yeah I know, police are human and therefore fallible and like everyone else they make mistakes and are not superheroes immune from the problems and short comings of being human.

So it goes, I suppose, even with our parents.

No, not with our parents. It simply can't be that way here.

They didn't protect us from an education system full of mediocrity, interested mostly, if not exclusively in creating people who "paid attention," "got along," and "fit."

They didn't protect us from a school system that created clones and sheep ready to follow and regurgitate yesterday's news and yesterday's ways.

They didn't concern themselves with us as individuals. They didn't help us as we looked for answers to difficult questions, and as we searched to feel a personal identity and a sense of happiness and worth.

They didn't protect us from educators and teachers who taught some kind of "party line," a line not at all interested in understanding, development and growth, but rather only with getting through and becoming a "part of the whole".

They didn't help us when the religions came calling. They didn't help us to see the flaws and the dangers of institutional religion.

They didn't prepare us for the lies, manipulation and the mass selling of a product that may be faulty. They didn't tell us that, like police, not all the religious people, religions and religious messages are not what they appear to be.

They didn't warn us to look closer, to be a little sceptical or unsure, or even to trust the ability to doubt.

Most disappointing, and heart breaking though, is that they did not teach us the power of the six ugly words.

My parents taught me to respect authority, to not be disrespectful, to keep in line and do what I was told.

They taught me to be good and do right and that I should and shouldn't until I was so full of rules and regulations that I simply became a product of things gone wrong.

Like so many others that I know or have known, I became a poster child for the Red Letters. I had should and shouldn't, right and wrong and good and bad down to a science.

Our parents, by and large, never took the time to see if it worked and made sense.

Was I, as a person, being cared for?
Did I have a spot that I could cherish?

Did I have any idea at all what made me tick?
Did I know how to relate to or understand others?
Did I know how to hear or listen?
Did I understand how to care for and about others? Did I learn how to care or gain a sense that I was part of a larger group?
Did I have the right to feel happy?

They didn't say to anybody,

This doesn't seem right.
Do you know what all these rules do to a person?
How will my child ever figure out what makes them happy?
All these rules and regulations promote guilt.
Do you know that we are not teaching them to think in new and different ways?
Do you know that yesterday's news is not necessarily the way to go forward?
Do you understand that religion separates us?
Do you know that we are inclined to judge each other?
Do you understand that my child is simply treated like a number here?
Don't you see that we are separating, segregating and not at all focusing on our common ground as people?

They never said "no" or "stop" or "redo it" or "get out" or "I have a responsibility," you know the responsibilities that all parents have towards their children.

The ones that they are just supposed to know.

Look, I am not a dreamer. I live in the same world as you and I have a child so I understand that it is very difficult. I do not expect every parent to take on the education system or the religious system by themselves; however, I do expect them as parents to pay attention and just because that's the way it was done before doesn't mean that's the way it ought to be done now.

Here is the real problem.

By and large, our parents, parents in general, whether they are twenty or eighty were in the same position that we are in. They were put on and taken hold of, by should and shouldn't, right and wrong and good and bad and they felt the pain and the pressure. They buckled, they hurt, and felt guilt, separation, anger, frustration, degradation and mostly they felt unhappy.

They took their mess, their pain and isolation, all of the garbage that the Red Letters did to them and they poured it on us.

Chin remembers his childhood with great pain and difficulty.

"My dad was so angry. He never said it, but I am sure he hated his life.

He drank a lot and when he drank he got even angrier. Sometimes he hit me and my sister.

I don't even remember why.

He was just so full of rage all of the time.

He never spoke of his pain, whatever it was, but when his parents came to visit, he got real quiet and drank a huge amount.

Sometimes when he thought he was alone, I would catch him crying. He always cried after his parents came to visit."

Juanita is hugely overweight. In fact her weight now threatens her life. One day, Juanita explained that her mother used to encourage her to eat excessively with her when she was a young girl.

"My mom would eat and cry. She would tell me in her weak moments that she ate because her parents were mean with her when she was a child. They called her names and I think that they might have even touched her. If I don't eat with my mom when she gets going, she screams at me and calls me names. Now look at me. I'm bigger than she is."

Chin's dad and Juanita's mom, unfortunately, are not unusual. Their lives were made messy by expectations or judgment or an inability to "fit" or "get it right" and as a result they became unhappy. Instead of fixing or trying to fix their mess they simply passed it on to their children and now the children live the parents' nightmare because the parents had no help, no resolution and no solution.

We kill our kids.

We allow the power and the expectations of the words I loath to consume us and then we pass it on.

Education and religion are on a mission. They are in the business of crowd control and in fact, people control. There is no stopping them. They have a job to do, to make us fit in, sheep, who follow prescriptions to a uniformed end. After all we can't have a bunch of disorganized, rule questioning, happy, aware people. Where would that leave us?

But our parents are supposed to know the code. You know, that stuff a few pages ago that spoke of the things parents are supposed to do.

Love us, care for us, protect us, sacrifice for us, help us...

They are not supposed to pass on their anger, their mess and their junk. They are not supposed to get so caught up in the ugliness of judgment, segregation, pettiness, and lack of awareness that they become the bearers of anger and spreaders of pain.

They are not supposed to kill their kids.

Get Off Me

I have chosen to single out education, religion and our parents as advocates, and in fact even ambassadors of the words that I so detest. They have been targeted as places that have given credence and power to words that might otherwise have no more power than a recipe for bread.

The truth is, that should and shouldn't, right and wrong and good and bad are common place and very influential in our daily lives.

In Western society, so many of us think nothing of using these words to get what we want, to promote guilt, encourage fear and cause pain. There is no need to be enrolled in school, attend religious services or visit your parents to receive the full force of the ugliness available. People in all kinds of regular everyday situations use "the six" as commonly as they would comment on the weather.

Friends offering loaded advice, co-workers deciding whether to hand out their "permission" or not, and family members, feeling that they have the right, an obligation almost, "to tell you". Others deciding for you, that you should or shouldn't do, think, or feel something, are common place.

I blame the institutions in our society for this rampant sanctimony. They powered up the words and then passed them out. It's almost like everyone carries a loaded gun, points it without any kind of discrimination or thought and shoots without remorse or consequence.

I told my friend that she shouldn't wear that sweater, it makes her look fat.
I told my co-worker that he should go to the movies instead of the opera. Opera is for losers.
I told my sister that she should get married in May. July is too hot for a wedding.

Are you kidding me?
Oh it only gets worse.

My friend is wrong to holiday in Europe. It's way too expensive.
It's only right to go to church on Sunday.
She asked him to marry her. How wrong is that?

See what I mean.

No good can come of that union.
Leaving home, that was just a bad move.
Good, he finally got rid of her.
She was no good for him anyway.

You're smiling because this is language that we use indiscriminately every day. The problem is that this is not choosing the wrong chocolate bar, a poor direction while searching for the new mall or an errant weather forecast. These words and the force with which they are used are damaging, hurtful and dangerous beyond imagination.

Peer pressure can be and usually is a horrible thing. The judgment and approval of those that we associate with is critical to our well-being. We may not recognize it, but the force of what others think, holds us, our behavior and maybe, most importantly, our happiness in it's very hands.

Most people are not strong enough to resist the garbage, guilt and manipulation heaped on them by others. Many people, regardless of their age or position in life, alter their attitude, appearance, point of view and behavior in general to suit a "demanding" opinion.

We have spent time looking at the power that others have over us. Unfortunately, what you think, even if it is thoughtless, is often important and has influence. Your anger, your vile point of view, your narrow mind and your insatiable need to criticize may be tools of disaster to those in your presence.

There was as famous modern French philosopher named Jean Paul Sartre. Sartre believed that hell, quite literally, was found "in the eyes of others". That we, each of us, with our judgments, our ridicule, criticism and our disapproval, have the power to make the lives of others so miserable that their existence is turned into a living hell. The look, the expression, or the comment on their own, had enough weight to push the recipient into despair and possibly into a decision to please that could be so devastating that an entire life might be altered and even lost.

Fortunately, for the next many pages we are going to look at ways to take away the power of the Red Letters. They can become as toothless as the time of day. In fact, with a little perspective and a few notions not previously entertained, we might even find some new life and have a little fun.

Part Two

Permission

Now What?

Certainly not all should and shouldn't, right and wrong and good and bad are necessarily to be thrown out. There are sometimes periods of essential agreement when it is important for the sake of clarity and maybe for the sake of common human ground to agree that we must come down on the side of being resolved and determined.

In those times we can suspend the criticism of the Red Letters and actually be direct and clear on a decision whose certainty is pretty much guaranteed. I mean guaranteed on a fundamental level of human decency that reaches beyond our learned and cultural understandings.

In a nutshell, there are certain things that require agreement from an innate human point of view. On these things we can use the ugly words, although here we use them from a position of actually caring about the greater or common good. It is bad to kill people unless there is a very good and justifiable reason. It is wrong to treat some people with less care and respect because of their race, religion or gender. We should try with all our resources to feed and shelter the world's poor.

The United Nations has a list like this with several more points. They have a clear list of should and shouldn't, good and bad and right and wrong that ought to be adhered to, for they reflect care and concern for all, beyond cultural points of view or bias. I know, even on these points, as basic as they are, we will never get unanimous agreement, however, this is the point where that innate thing that I speak of clicks in.

Don't like the word innate? No problem. Let's just say basic human decency.

So this brings us to a new place. The six horrible words have been dragged into the light and now, maybe for the first time they are exposed and you will see them differently. See them for what they truly are.

Ok, maybe we are ready for a change. What do we do now?

Thanks for the information, even thanks for the lesson, but now here I sit with my Red Letters exposed and no real options. At least before I had some idea what I was up to.

Now we are simply supposed to avoid causing guilt, pain, manipulation and separation by being sensitive to a group of words that hurt others.

"I don't want to hurt others but I have lost the use of six very familiar words and I am still unhappy, unsure and unfulfilled."

I have a new word, one that will occupy us for the next while.

A word with such possibility you will, I think, be thrilled to forget the harmful six, and gladly replace them with this one new, hopeful, exciting and very freeing word.

Permission.

For every bit of damage that the miserable six contributed to and for every bit of "how did I get here," permission will offer a solution, an out and an option. The biggest thing to keep in mind with permission, however, is that it too has several consequences attached to it. It must be used carefully and does not offer a free ride on any level.

Just as the Red Letters are generally words of cowardice, permission is a word that requires great courage, personal commitment and truly an investment in you.

Robert called me yesterday. Yes, the same Robert.

"I thought a great deal about our last conversation. You know the permission stuff. I can do things differently. I can take some chances and make some changes. How do I undo my mess and my hurt? What is it exactly that I can do differently? Where do I start?"

Well Robert, my friend, let us have a look.

Something Completely New

When I think of permission three things come immediately to my mind. Why do I need permission, how do I get permission and permission for what?

The quick and easy answer, and maybe in the end the only one that matters for why we need permission, is that permission is exactly the opposite of the words that I have been railing on and warning you against. Permission is at the very other end of the spectrum and therefore needs our examination and our attention.

For every act of malice, judgment and separation there is a trail to should and shouldn't, right and wrong and good and bad. Each time we seek to belittle or decide who is in and who is out, who is us and who is them, there are the six words that divide, reach into our insides and pull out our worst.

We've been through this. "I can and do decide where you fit, who you are, what your worth is, how your actions measure up and if I am going to harm you and by how much." In that moment, I determine whether you ought to be considered, accepted, rejected or even put in harm's way.

This approach simply doesn't work. It divides, causes pain, guilt and fear and has the ability because it is harsh, cruel and void of compassion, to hurt others and therefore ourselves. I don't mean to sound like a cliché, but occasionally they are true.

For every time that I as an individual, hurt or demean another, I hurt or lessen myself. My effort towards the world around me and therefore my effort toward others is a direct reflection of who and what I am.

There are some, I am sure, who have a problem with this connection.

"I am judgmental, mean and small minded. I am happy to categorize and limit others and I have no trouble with my point of view and my words causing harm.

My superior, angry, hurtful position in life is just fine with me. I am not interested in change, growth or self-examination."

I have, I am sorry to say, known a number of people over the years who are very happy to be petty, ugly and cruel. They are people who, in fact, even delight in causing difficulty for others. I have also come to see that many people act the way they do because they see no alternative for themselves. They believe their programming, and their path and they are resigned to be "in it" and live it with the careless attitude of "I am who I am."

Anne once told me a sad story. She said that she could not change.

"I am too old and I have been this way for years. All of the members of my family were racists. I know it

sounds ridiculous but I was raised that way. I have always thought that way and I am too old to change. Even if I wanted to change, I wouldn't know how. I wouldn't have a clue. Do you have any idea how hard it would be to do things differently after more than sixty years?"

Permission brings us away from all of the small minded, gossip-column stuff.

Permission causes you to challenge ignorance.

Those who reject permission to examine themselves might be happy to say, like Anne, "Hey look at the way we are, sheep, following and carrying on mindlessly with little or no thought and certainly no regard for others or even ourselves."

They claim that the crowd and the majority are correct and they scream, "Not me, I am not an individual. I am just like everyone else."

If on the other hand being a cog in a wheel, a fish in a school, a mindless, thoughtless machine are not the kind of self descriptive words that you find attractive. If this is not the image that you want to be associated with and not how you want to be seen or how you want to live your life, then permission is for you.

First and foremost and this is massive:

Permission will allow you to do things differently. It will allow you to examine yourself, your life, your choices, your point of view and the way you carry on, on a daily basis.

Why do you need permission? Well, because it is the first and definitely the most important step to doing things, pretty much all things, differently.

How do I get permission? It really sounds silly but you have to allow it. You have to look around and say, "No. I don't like the way things are and I don't like the way I am and I am not going to do that or be that anymore."

Those who know a great deal about change, personal change, will tell you that "the first step is admitting": Admitting that you need to do things differently, see things differently and be a different person. All of this requires permission to say, "Hold on. Stop. I want to try something new." I know it sounds simple. Say the magic words and it all begins.

Unfortunately it's not quite that easy. The road is long and very difficult because usually we have years of training to do things the old way and the old way is easy to understand.

Femi came from Africa several years ago. For him the culture shock was immense. Almost everything was a huge problem. For months he sat in his room, venturing out as little as possible. He could not cope with all the changes. He tried to remain an African in a non-African world.

I clearly remember the day he said to me, "I want to do it differently. I want to learn new ways."

Permission is a gift and as it is with most gifts there are two very important sides involved. First the gift needs to be offered and second it has to be accepted. You can offer your friend the gift of learning a new dance forever and with all sincerity and excitement, however, until she is ready to accept the offer, it's all only words that sit there waiting to be collected, tried on and appreciated.

Anne had clearly been offered the gift of changing her point of view, permission, if you will, to try to do things differently. She decided that her age and her comfort level prevented her from ever receiving the gift of something new.

This is the backbone of permission.

First decide (and this can take a long time and certainly requires a lot of courage) to do things differently. Decide that you are tired of the same old rut, the same old, same old. Then, if possible, find someone who sees things and maybe does things differently. Find someone who, if you will, offers you the gift of something new. This sounds huge, it doesn't have to be. Speak to the person at work who eats different food and find out about it. Join some new co-workers on a night out.

Try a different kind of food or a new kind of clothing. Go to the kind of movie that you might have previously avoided. Read a book, turn off the TV. It's all about being open enough to try something new, something different. It's all about the permission to try. To say maybe, or yeah, or I'm going to risk and try to do it differently or think about it differently.

Permission starts small, you will be surprised.

Self Care

Now that we have seen clearly that so many of the rules, the very things that we base our lives and our daily activity on are seriously flawed, we might want to re-examine the whole thing.

It's no secret now that so much of what we base our perspective and our foundation on is suspect. The Red Letters are, it would seem, at the very core of deciding who we are, how we live and what we see as important.

When someone disapproves of me I will change to make them happy or I will become defensive and fight with them. Considering their point of view is unlikely for me.

When I encounter something "different," a person, place or thing, I am likely to react with distain and distrust and say something that is negative.

When given the chance I become judgmental and small-minded.

I love my routine and become suspect or unhappy when there is a change.

I easily find myself deciding how others ought to act, think and even live their lives.

I like rules and regulations and enjoy quoting things that I have been told are good or bad, right or wrong.

I like to be popular. I do not like to rock the boat and what others think about me is very important to my happiness.

These are just a few examples of how those ugly words shape and mold so many of us and how they hold our actions and our attitudes.

Now that they have been exposed and now that we see them for what they are, they may have lost some of their credibility. Maybe now we can risk and consider other options.

In the last section I asked the final important question on permission, that is, permission for what? I think first and foremost we need to give ourselves permission to care for ourselves differently than we have.

It's really the same as doing things differently. First, say to yourself, "I want to change and I want to improve. I am tired of my rut, my routine, my point of view and this big bag of junk that I carry around every day. In fact, I am, if I say it quietly and to myself, tired of me, my life and my whole situation." The Red Letters should and shouldn't, right and wrong and good and bad have programmed us through years of being threatened and pounded on by them.

They have trained us to act, react and live in certain ways. First we must decide its ok to care for ourselves differently than we did yesterday and we must decide that we no longer have to be cemented, committed or bound to the story or the act that held us together yesterday.

Start small. Consider allowing a small voice inside to say,

I can see it differently.
I can try it differently.
I can do it differently.
I do not have to sing the same song today that I sang yesterday.
I can and I will try something new.
I am willing to care for myself. I am not a robot, or a trained seal. I am not here to please others only. I want to feel different, maybe even happier.
I will not spend my whole life doing as others would have me do.
I want to care for myself.

Start small. Try something that is new and desired.

George found himself a product of television. He confessed to me one day that he watched at least eight hours of TV every day.

"I hate that my entire life revolves around the TV but I have no idea what else to do. When I asked him what he wanted to do he looked at me with an expression of complete mystery. What should I do?"

"Think about it George, something will come to you but try and do with less TV."

I saw George only four days later. He was ecstatic.

"I only have two, two TV's. I gave three of them away. You wouldn't believe it but I used to have five. There was nowhere that I could go without finding another screen. I am embarrassed to tell you that I had a small TV in the bathroom. I don't need to live like this. I don't need to be a fool who has no life and only the opinion of the screen. I was so popular at work because I could relate to almost everyone. They all have a favorite show and I could talk about all of them.

Look I am carrying a book. I had time for TV and I haven't read a book for years. I now have time for anything. I was too damn busy being a sheep, nothing but a consumer."

George gave himself the option to receive permission to consider doing things a little differently. A book may not change his world but it is a start. George said I will care for myself in a new way and I will live tomorrow a little differently than I lived yesterday. Permission for self-care is not the same thing at all as permission to be selfish.

The person who goes to the gym, the spa, the bar, for endless hours of me time is not involved in self care but rather selfish indulgence.

Self care is about finding something that you wish to change and improve and addressing it. Spending your money on an expensive car is not self-care. It may be a fun, maybe even a worthwhile thing to do but self-care is recognizing a weakness or a need in your life and trying through permission to fill that weakness or need.

Like George, I want to give myself permission to exercise because exercise will likely make me healthier and therefore feel better about myself.

I want to meet new people because I am stuck in a rut. I want to give myself permission to dress differently because I want to tell others that I have a new self-image.

I give myself permission to eat differently, think differently, and interact differently with people. All of these things allow me to experience myself and life from a new perspective and as a result I am becoming new.

This is self-care.

Jack was tired of eating meat. He could no longer give himself permission to continue to eat the way he had for years.

"It was such a struggle. My friends and family questioned me and in some cases even made fun of me. Let's be honest, I wasn't doing things the same way, the same as them and so I was, I guess, calling into question what they were doing. I never preached or converted or judged. I simply said no thank you. I do not wish to eat meat or fish. Some people took my decision about me and my choices as a personal insult. Wow! One little decision and I felt uncomfortable, had to put up with ridicule, odd

glances, strange questions and I even lost two "friends." I really just wanted to do things differently."

Jack was involved in self-care. He gave himself permission to consider things differently and do things differently. He suffered some consequences but was determined to try something new.

Jack did not need to be exactly the same today that he was yesterday.

The Big P

I know, see a new kind of film, have lunch with someone new, buy a book, or even stop eating meat. Are you kidding me? All these amount to cosmetic changes. Nothing more than simple things that anybody can do at anytime. Absolutely, you are correct, none of these things on their own amount to much of anything at all.

We all make choices daily that are a little out of the ordinary and we all do things a bit differently from time to time. Surely, these "new directions" are nothing to get excited about.

The choices are completely irrelevant. The important thing is that new ideas and possibilities appeared in the minds and lives of those involved and new possibilities were desired and sought after.

It doesn't matter if you chose white wine instead of red, mountain climbing instead of sitting behind a desk, or going naked in public instead of keeping your clothes on.

It only matters that you have come to a place where you recognize that what was, is no longer what you need and you must seek a change.

Yesterday's message, yesterday's song or story is no longer the thing that I want or need to tell or be a part of.

My life has gotten to the point where I require new options and new possibilities.

I want to see it differently, understand it differently and maybe most importantly I want to do it differently. Really that's all that matters.

Maybe you're questioning things about your life or even life itself. Maybe you realize that things don't work anymore the way you thought they worked in the past or maybe you have been struck by some kind of "life changing lightening."

It doesn't matter.

All that really matters is that you, all on your own, completely of your own volition have found a place that says "I see new possibilities." I like that and I want to turn the square a little and see for the first time that, wow, it's a diamond. In this case a simple changing of the square may be absolutely, completely, life changing and profound. It is at the moment of realizing possibilities that we break out, even if only a little, from the grasp of the Red Letters.

They have no patience for change, no tolerance for new and they hate possibilities.

With years of should and shouldn't, right and wrong and good and bad, we have been trained and indoctrinated down to the last letter. That training has no room for possibilities, no room for anything beyond what we have been sold as "truth" and the way we "must be." I am certain that anytime there is a clear conscious change from the old to something else, anytime we question the power of the Red Letters, for a new, thoughtful place, we have begun to turn the square a few degrees and now desire to see the diamond.

Change can be very risky, but this is the start of permission and how to accept and use it to change your life.

Let me show you.

Raymond is a man who I have known for nearly twenty years. He is conservative, quiet, thoughtful and certainly what I would call a person very much aware of the power of the Red Letters.

Some time ago he and I were speaking of the ills of society and he broke into a rant or at least a rant for him about people throwing their garbage on the street.

"Don't they see this is their world too?
Don't they know that we all have to exist together?"

I agreed and we parted company wishing the world and those in it were more thoughtful and insightful.

Three days later Raymond called me in what seemed like a panic.

"I need to see you. Can you please come by my office, I have some news."

Raymond was beside himself.

"I can't believe I did it but I did, I made a difference. Do you remember our conversation about garbage? Yesterday I was driving home and I was at the light at the corner, waiting to turn left and the car behind me was also waiting to turn left.
I happened to look in my side mirror and they were throwing small bags of garbage out of the window onto the street.
I don't know what happened to me, but I snapped. I got out of the car and confronted them.
I told them that if they didn't pick up the garbage I wasn't going to move my car.
By this time there were other cars behind them and they were honking their horns.
The "garbage people" got out of their car and picked up the garbage.
I know, I know, once they got down the street they probably called me names and threw their garbage out of the window again.
I don't care.
I only care that I said to myself I can't live like this anymore.
I can't continue to be meek and rule abiding and non confrontational.
I want to make a difference."

Raymond was on fire.

The really interesting thing here for me wasn't that he got the courage to stand up and confront. That alone was fantastic, but his excitement to be a new person was inspiring and infectious. He was now a changed man who saw new possibility and decided to live it.

I can tell you that since that day, almost four years ago, Raymond does many things differently. He is only a mere reflection of the man he used to be. He sees things differently and acts in new and exciting ways.

Raymond took the inspiration of "I am not going to be the guy who always plays by the same old rules" and he took steps from there to change his life.

I see Raymond regularly and he is barely recognizable. He appreciates his lot and is often telling people how he sees life differently since he saw new possibilities for who he is and how he acts.

Raymond loves to tell the garbage story. Don't get me wrong Raymond did not turn into a bully, screaming at people on the street whose actions he disagreed with. He simply decided that he had to take more responsibility for the world around him. Raymond works a night a week for a local charity, gives his employees more vacation days, spends time teaching English to those who have trouble with the language. He has turned into a very kind man who doesn't mind breaking the rules on occasion.

Raymond saw the possibility of living differently and he seized it. It all began with a moment of passion that brought him face to face with realities about his life that he had to change.

Condalisa is a woman who I met recently. She told me how both her parents had died within a few months of each other. She told me how she felt like an orphan.

"After my mom and dad died it all seemed useless, ridiculous and pointless to me.

What on earth was life about? All the meaning I had in the world had died with my mom and dad. I know it sounds silly. I'm thirty three years old and I have no idea what to do with myself. Within weeks I began to question all of the things I thought were certain.

It wasn't long before I found myself re evaluating so many parts of my life. I don't want to be the person that I was before. I lived in some kind of dream world.

My parents were angry and suspicious of everything and everybody. I loved them very much but had, even without knowing, become them. A few months after they died I went out on a couple of dates. All I could do was be critical of these men. They were not up to my parents' standard and they had so many imperfections.

One day one of these men called me and said maybe I needed to open my eyes and try to see things differently. Maybe I could cut people a bit of slack and stop judging everyone. I spent two months locked up in the house. I went to work and bought groceries, but basically I became a hermit. I found myself reading the paper or watching TV feeling anger and contempt for everyone and everything. I don't know where all the rules came from but I was sure full of them.

Things are different now. I get out and I try to appreciate people for who and what they are. I had no idea that people could be so much fun. You wouldn't believe the things I try now. You wouldn't believe the things I say and think. I am not the old Condalisa."

Condalisa's parents had to leave her alone, lonely, angry and lost for her to figure out that she had some options. She calls it her epiphany. She believes that her parents' death was partially, at least, to "wake her up" and to see that she had other options, other possibilities for her life.

These are big time permission stories. They are more than a book, or a new kind of shoes. These self-examination stories are at the heart of permission. Permission to look and mostly, permission to see. These are not simply "feel good" and I finally "got it" stories. These are stories where people have said to themselves "out with the old." That is the very thing needed to grasp possibilities and permission.

How It Feels

I had a good friend a number of years ago who was an oncologist (a cancer doctor). He would encounter so many situations in life, shrug his shoulders and say "it doesn't matter." He would say this about almost any life situation short of a true medical emergency or horribly bad news. "How is it that you are so unfazed by so many of the things going on around you?"
He would shrug and say "they really don't matter."

"Whether you buy a blue car or a red car, spill soup on your pants, don't get to the bus or have a fight with your partner, it's all nonsense, not important and it really doesn't matter. We spend so much time trapped by the small, unimportant things."

The power of his words "ripped me" and through them I began to see possibilities, possibilities that I have now held and nurtured for years. With his wisdom I felt such a huge relief. I am certain that I could feel the weight of my worries lift off me. Here was a friend and a man who I trusted helping me to put things into perspective very quickly and simply with the phrase "it doesn't matter."

Allow me to pass that same perspective and permission on to you.

There are so very many things that do matter but so often they have nothing to do with the things that we are heavily invested in. The words that I have called out are nothing more than limiting factors to our growth, our intelligence and our happiness and therefore the happiness of others and they have no interest in letting go of you. They have a huge interest in "it really matters." They would have us fret all the time, non-stop, over the smallest things until we become paralyzed, frustrated, angry and lost.

Did I do the right thing?
Am I a good boy?
Is it right to?
Am I wrong when I?
Should I or shouldn't I?

The list is endless and the worries and the accompanying paralysis are never-ending. Charles' (my friend the oncologist) words are freeing, hopeful and completely the enemy of the Red Letters. They would have us seek permission and possibility and strip away the petty, the routine, the mundane and the bucket of garbage that we carry around with us full of should and shouldn't, right and wrong and good and bad.

Michael is a kind man who was raised in a very strict family and he worries a lot. His entire upbringing was somewhat puritanical and controlled by should and shouldn't, right and wrong and good and bad. He loves to hear me tell him that he does not have to be that way or that guy any more.

"Michael, let it go.
You don't need that any more.
The anger, the frustration, the rules and regulations are yesterday's story.
You can, if you like, begin a new story and you can begin it today.
The guy from the strict family is who you were yesterday.
He, however, does not have to be the guy you are today.
Michael, let it go.
You don't need it any more.
You don't have to be weighed down with yesterday's news, yesterday's stories and yesterday's pain.
Please be responsible but be happy.
Michael, do what you need to do and please be who and what you need to be."

Michael loves the words, feels the power, weeps when I say them and thanks me for the permission to be something new, different and free.

The Red Letters hate me.

When I Was A Child

I remember clearly as a child the power of permission. I remember the feeling of absolute joy, relief, happiness and unlimited possibility when my parents would, on rare occasions, tell me that the choices were endless and I was in complete control.

I can still recall going to the local fair, looking wondrously at all the rides and games and saying to my mother or father, "What should I do first?"

It was rare, but happened occasionally, based on their level of tolerance, patience and (I figured this out later) likely the way they were feeling about each other, that they would say, "Do whatever you like." "We are going to be here for two hours, do whatever makes you happy."

The disbelief and the real wonder of somehow being in control of my very own two hours was a feeling that I can still vividly remember. There were so many choices, so many wonderful possibilities. I remember other times like that. Times when I was given a small amount of money and told to go to the corner store to buy candy.

One parent or both were feeling generous, kind or maybe guilty (I figured that one out later too) and they would give me permission to take my money to the store to do exactly as I chose.

I was free and the feeling stays with me all these years later.

Even as I write these words I smile and feel warm.

For a few minutes every once in a while I got to choose and I got to decide.

I had no one to please or disappoint and there were essentially no rules.

Children need rules in order to feel safe and know how to act and respond but they also need the feeling of freedom and permission so that they might bask in the wonder and peace of not making a wrong choice.

Where permission is concerned there is only one rule. It's a good rule, one that the Western world at least, invests in and holds close to the very heart (pardon the pun) of society.

Hippocrates was considered the father of Western medicine and in honor of his place in history; medical schools have adopted an oath that he is credited with. The part of the oath that most interests me are the words "above all, do no harm." Permission can be revelled in, enjoyed and celebrated as long as harm is not intended.

This permission thing is not, now or ever, about caring for you at the expense of others. Neither is it a question of "Do what you like or need to do, and to hell with the consequences or the pain caused to others."

On the contrary, permission is that which provides us with a sense of freedom to pursue happiness, and happiness is impossible to achieve at the expense of others.

Anyone who becomes happy at another's expense is only able to look to their needs and that alone negates being happy.

Like the happy, free feeling that I can recall as a child, I have known permission as an adult. Sometimes my need to do as I wanted was so strong that I made a mess of the situation for others. In the end, my permission only caused me to hurt and recoil.

For me, I need to constantly check and re-check that I am not insensitive to the place of others.

Of course every action has consequences and reactions. I have no problem here, however, when your actions run contrary to the well- being of others then you might want to consider your motivation.

We must make difficult choices from time to time. Choices that, of course, will not be approved by everyone around us and choices that may inevitably cause others harm and pain.

This is simply the cost of being in relationships.

My point is that when permission becomes selfish and only considers me and what I need, then permission has become more important than relationships.

Of course, there will be times that we must forge ahead because others are unable or unwilling to see what might be good or even best for us.

A good starting point is often, how will granting myself permission, emancipation, if you will, affect those around me.

If the answer is, "with great difficulty" then I suggest communication and negotiation.

If that is out of the question and your peace of mind and personal happiness is at stake then you may want to move ahead, providing you are not malicious, and be prepared to bear the cost of your choices. Unfortunately, not all choices will be appreciated and recognized as worthwhile. Sometimes sacrifices have to be made.

When you get there you will have to decide if staying "in line" while keeping others calm is desired, or if rocking the boat in order to achieve peace is the thing to do.

Jasmine was very unhappy, distressed and disturbed by a series of unhappy events in her life and involved in a marriage that was miserable.

She embarked on a series of sexual affairs with a number of different people.

Her adventures had two purposes. They were a distraction to her misery and they were also a misguided attempt to feel happy.

Jasmine gave herself permission to make a mess.

She might have been better off giving herself permission to address her painful family situation and her failed marriage. She might have given herself permission to address the cause of her unhappiness rather than making herself, her family and many other people more miserable.

Whether Jasmine had sexual relations with many people is not the issue. That brings us back to should and shouldn't, right and wrong and good and bad. The issue is about giving ourselves permission to tackle the central issues so that we can go forward feeling new and confident that yesterday's baggage and yesterday's mess are cared for, dealt with and made powerless.

To address a misuse of alcohol by beginning to misuse drugs is hardly focusing on the problem. Permission is so very powerful and potentially so wonderful that we must not only pursue it but we must respect it.

One of the very best places to consider beginning is to grant yourself the permission to be honest and to begin a quest to be who and what you are, whatever that may be.

Still today, many years away from the few cents at the candy store, I am overwhelmed by the power and beauty of the feeling "do what you need to do and be who you need to be."

Give up the person you were yesterday and try being the person you need to be today.

Risk and search for the courage to say "I know the rules but on this point I choose to ignore them."

I am going to know the red letters and ignore them because they are not me.

On this point and on this occasion I am going to be me, follow my needs and find the courage to be as honest, open and free with myself and others as I possibly can be.

Today I will be different, and whether others like it or not, my new considered ways are not open to their judgment or their approval.

Deiter was miserable. He lived by his family's rules for years and finally had no choice in his mind but to tell them that he had fallen in love with a man. For years he had listened to them poke fun at gays and lesbians, not knowing that Deiter was, in fact, a homosexual. For years he bit his tongue and hid his true feelings pretending to be something that he was not.

He told me that family gatherings were especially painful. "My family had no interest in the feelings or convictions of others. They were sanctimonious, judgmental and very small. Essentially, it was their way or no way at all."

One Thanksgiving, he could take the pettiness and judgment of his family no more. Deiter lost control in the middle of a large family dinner, stood up with his turkey dinner plate in his hand and threw it at the wall. After getting the attention of the group, in a spectacular manner, he announced that he was gay and left.

I met Deiter two years later when he was dying from cancer. Amazingly, he was able to tell me that the happiest two years of his life were the last two and that, even now, even on his death bed he felt relieved and happy at his choice and the painful way that he broke the news to his family. His honesty was harmful to others, but necessary for his freedom and future.

So throw the plate if you need to. Remember, however, whether you live life on your terms with permission and freedom to be what you need to be, or spend it living up to the expectations of others, try to be authentic, honest and determined.

Remember to accept the consequences of your choices (in other words be an adult) while doing the least amount of harm possible.

Yesterday

I am different today than I was yesterday.

I recognize the difference, I like being different, look forward to being different and I definitely celebrate the changes, small and large, that takes place within me on a daily basis.

Of course, some of the changes are small and very subtle, so small in fact that they are not recognizable and at other times I move more in a day than I have in a year.

For me the thought of today being somehow different than yesterday, and tomorrow being potentially something new all over again is so exciting, so life giving, that it keeps me alive and hopeful.

I awaken each morning wondering what the day will bring. I am not curious about something new for breakfast or new products on the shelf of the local store. Rather, learning something about me, my environment and those that I interact with is important beyond words.

Did I learn something new?
Did I consider something in a new way?
Have I found a way to turn the square and see a diamond?
Did my understanding, my compassion and my humanity grow?

Am I a "better person" somehow today than I was yesterday?
Have I learned more about my spirit, my psyche, my intellect, my emotions or my animal than I knew yesterday?
Am I more in touch today than I was yesterday?
Am I a better friend, parent, partner, human being than I was yesterday?
Am I committed to finding growth and therefore change in my life each and every day?

I want you to know that this "dance" that I do, often has steps that I do not understand and that in this "dance" I get tangled and even fall a great deal. To all that I reference my friend Charles (the cancer doctor) and say "it doesn't matter." All that really matters is that I like to learn, grow, change, laugh at myself and show up each day to "dance" all over again.

I decided some years ago that life was definitely a trip, often with a destination unknown that requires me to simply show up for the ride, keep my eyes and ears open and want to learn and develop as I go.

If you believe, or want to believe that yesterday is gone and that with its passing the things that we carried with us, the stories that we told and the "markings" that we had are all things that have the potential not to follow us to today;. then you truly have the opportunity each and every day to learn something new about yourself, your world and those you come into contact with.

You also, absolutely, have the chance to play your life out differently and, silly as it sounds, the chance to be something new and wonderful.

Is there something about today that was so terrific, so fantastic that you need to replay it in its entirety again tomorrow?

Do you need to see the same film over and over again? Surely using that analogy you would demand your money back.

I have seen this.

I do not need to see it again.

For some people the thought of change is frightening to the point of paralysis.

In fact, the Red Letters and those who strongly support them are not happy with change.

If there is a continual evolution, how can we decide what's right and wrong, good and bad or for that matter in a changing world, a learning, developing place, how do we even should and shouldn't each other?

Indeed what was the standard yesterday is now under scrutiny today.

Barely a day goes by that I don't shake my head and wonder "What was I thinking?"

Let me tell you about two women that I know right now, who are vastly different in their perspective and their approach to life.

Roxanne is a very bright, quick, very aggressive, angry, young woman. She is not particularly tolerant, has a short fuse and certainly does not suffer fools gladly.

Roxanne is also damaged, tainted by her life experience, to the point of being an enormous cynic and skeptic.

We are all, of course, wounded or damaged on some level. Roxanne, however, displays her scars more prominently than others.

We have a standing disagreement. She believes passionately that the world and those in it are cruel and ugly and that it is pretty much "everyone for themselves."

I hear and understand her point of view (sometimes buy into it) but prefer to focus on the positives and the signs of hope.

One hope that I cling to is the ability to change and to not have yesterday follow us to tomorrow.

I offer Roxanne the change argument. I implore her to see the possibilities and the potential that exists within people in general and therefore, maybe even especially, within herself.

Roxanne can only recall yesterday.

She sees and feels her bitter life experiences and still reverberates over pain and ugliness seen or experienced from her past.

What Roxanne puts out is nasty and off-putting and as a result she will fulfill her own sense of the world.

It takes a great deal of courage to engage her and so, most simply placate her or ignore or avoid her all together.

Besides anger Roxanne carries a great deal of judgment with her. She is quick to determine the worth of others, to see the "good and bad," "right and wrong" around her. Her think armor is full of should and shouldn't. She has no time and no patience for change or for possibilities and permission.

Christina on the other hand is very different.

She is full of enthusiasm for tomorrow. She is so eager for change and betterment, optimism and hope that she ought to really be on a poster somewhere.

Christina has sustained a good deal of damage during her life too.

She, like Roxanne, suffers the effects of many things gone sour and many periods of pain and misery.

Unlike Roxanne, however, Christina looks to do things differently, better, if you will, each day.

In fact she is so keen "to get it right" or improve her lot, that she openly seeks suggestions on relationships, human decency and interaction regularly.

Both of these woman are in their thirties, both are interesting to be with and both have a great deal to offer.

Christina has little time for yesterday. She celebrates what she "got right," enjoys her successes and the things that have made her feel good and she comes to the world each and every day looking to grow, change and further develop.

Christina looks for possibilities and she takes the permission to grow and change and runs with it.

Roxanne is so full of loathing and so committed to yesterday's view of the world and I suppose her entrenched self perception, that change for her is very difficult.

She drags her ugly bag of anger around with her and she becomes it. Roxanne is not yet ready to give up on yesterday and forge a new tomorrow.

These women represent two divergent points of view. They approach life differently and as a result experience life differently.

Their lives speak to my point.

Of course we are not new each day; we carry our "accumulation" around with us. We are, though, creatures of posture, and depending on how we face ourselves and the world we meet, we will impact and be impacted on.

I am not suggesting for a minute that we toss our past out, that would be impossible. Rather, take the position that yesterday does not necessarily control today and that it can have even less control over tomorrow.

This position frustrates the Red Letters, keeps them off guard and begins to strip them of their power.

I know for a fact that Christina asks herself daily,

Did I try something new?
Did I try to learn something I did not know?
Was I friendlier, kinder, and gentler?
Did I care about those I came into contact with?
Have I more insight today than yesterday?
Did I dismantle even a piece of the ugly words?

Maybe more importantly I am certain that she asks,

Did I repeat yesterday's mistakes?
Did I catch myself being hard or arrogant or brutal?
Have I lost something today that I recognized that I needed to lose yesterday?
Did I listen, learn and pay attention to the lessons around me?
Did I move further away from harsh, judgmental and us and them?

Yesterday brings us to where we are. It does not have to take us where we are going.

Permission allows possibilities, take them and consider tomorrow differently.

Relationships

Permission to be new and different is of course about us, it is about who we are, how we act and react and what we choose to do with our time and our lives. At the end, permission is a fantastically useful psychological tool that, if handled well, will lead us to question our choices, our motivations and our very lives.

Of course, as we look at us and the things that we want or need, we are brought face to face with the words I fight with.

Can I make choices that might be contradictory to my upbringing?

What if I go against the grain? Is my happiness, my life, more important than tradition and the wisdom of the group?

Do I have the courage and the confidences to resist the pressures around me and pursue the things that I feel are important?

Will I be able to deal with and face any possible backlash from others?

Most importantly, though, is the question, "How do I manage my life and my needs when it comes to others?"

Here I mean specifically those that we interact with, and relate to. Facing "the group" or the society is one thing, but learning to deal with, work with and grow with your family and friends is a whole different thing.

I have always thought that the idea of long term or even "lifetime" relationships was a very odd and extremely difficult thing. The thought of having a friend that you met in high school for instance, who continues to be your friend until your advanced years, or even until you die, seems almost impossible to me.

Even more unrealistic is the idea of keeping the same partner from the point where you begin your union, until you separate by death. That might be, thirty, forty, fifty or even more years later. "Till death do us part."

I have long had trouble seeing how two people can meet at a certain point in their life where they are compatible and somehow remain compatible for many years to come.

People change and grow. We move in different directions, find different things that motivate and drive us. We are influenced by forces, sometimes beyond our control, that cause us to develop and change and we very often do this all by ourselves. How on earth can you have this kind of change and movement happening over many years by two people and yet still have them remain together, compatible and happy?

In my mind and in my experience the only way is by permission.

It is essential and absolutely critical to any long term relationship that three factors exist.

You must be committed to communication. You must be committed to being honest, and you must be able to use permission for yourself and offer it as a gift to those closest to you. I will not digress into couple counseling, however, there may be something to be learned here.

If you do not communicate and if you are not honest with yourself and those closest to you, then you will live a lie, a mess, and be in a situation that is bound to fail. Your inability to be open will cause you and those around you an enormous amount of pain.

If you are able to find a way to risk, say what's on your mind, express what you need and where you are, then and only then, do you stand the remotest of chances of making a friendship or personal relationship of any kind really work.

Gerry and Bev have been together for more years than most people have been alive.

From all I could see, on so many levels, they could barely tolerate each other. They were, however, attached to the idea of being together and had, I am fairly sure, no idea how to not be together.

Gerry and Bev became nothing more than a bad habit.

Honesty was out of the question, someone might tell "the truth," someone might get hurt or offended and then it would be a real mess. The quiet mess would be out in the open and everyone would know that Gerry and Bev were a disaster.

They would not want that. They decided, no doubt, by default that they would simply "suck it up," get on with it and pretend.

Well, that's what people do isn't it? I am being a little flippant, but Gerry and Bev are not unique. They are, I think, the norm.

Let me show you how permission comes in. Let me show you how it can make even a long term relationship work, be fun, interesting, exciting and very possible.

Sometimes it is difficult to understand that people, who are committed to each other, whether they are solid friends or loving partners, can hold the happiness of the other in their hands and choose to dole it out sparingly, only as they see fit, or not at all. How is it that I can say, "You my friend or my love are so very important to me, yet your happiness is at my discretion? In fact, I may not want you to be happy, because your happiness may infringe on me. Your well being may cause me to feel insecure, threatened or miserable."

This is the point that I was making earlier. How do I love you as my friend or my partner, my sister or my brother, yet attach conditions to your growth, freedom, self discovery and changing development?

We all know these situations. Let me choose a very simple, non- threatening example.

James hates it when Sally goes out with the girls because he is left behind, he feels deserted and insecure that Sally is having fun without him. Or maybe worse, maybe Sally is "unprotected" and available to be gazed at by other men. Maybe Sally might even enjoy the "freedom" or the attention.

James therefore limits Sally's time out with her friends because he is not settled in their relationship. He claims that he wants her happy and fulfilled, yet her fulfillment had better be on his terms or at least terms that he can comfortably grasp.

Sally needs to be honest and open with James.

"I am an adult, I need certain stimulations in my life and I need to feel that time out with my friends is not only allowed but encouraged and celebrated by you."

James wants Sally to be happy, but her happiness needs to have agreed limits, I have no problem with that. The limits, however, must be regularly re-examined and renegotiated.

The thing is, that both Sally and James change. Their needs are certainly not the same as when they met, even if they only met a few months ago. They grow, evolve and become different as time goes on. It is possible that when they met, Sally did not spend much time with her friends but now she needs to do that.

See what I mean? How can these two people stay together and be happy? James needs one thing and Sally needs another. As far as I can tell, and this is a very simple example, James and Sally have a real problem.

"Are you kidding me?" you might be saying. This is nothing more than simple white bread stuff for a couple. Maybe, but this very tension is what easily exists between any two people involved in a long term relationship.

One person wants and needs one thing and the other person is uncomfortable and needs something else. The only way for one person to not limit the needs and wants of the other and the only way for one person to continue to grow and develop with the other, is for there to be constant communication, honesty and permission.

"You're evolution scares me, I no longer know where I fit. I feel frightened that I have lost my spot or to be more honest, my influence in your life. I don't want to lose you and I don't like that you get attention elsewhere."

The moment that James speaks these words as a starting point, Sally knows exactly what she is dealing with. She now has the ball and the chance to be equally honest.

"I need time with my friends. I need time away from you and to be honest, I like some of the attention that I get when I am with women only."

And so it goes. Sally and James now have a live one on their hands. It stays active, exciting and a place for wonderful growth, learning and communication as long as they stay honest with each other.

Where it moves to all out fantastic, life-giving hope for a strong relationship that has so many possibilities is when permission is given. Imagine this.

"Sally I want you happy.
I want to journey with you wherever that is.
I want to discover with you and grow with you.
When things become uncomfortable for me and they will, I will need your help.
Please teach me what you need and how best to respond to you and I will do my best.
I am weak and fragile and I get lost in my own fears and inabilities.
There will be times that your needs conflict with mine and then I will need you to be patient and negotiate with me.

As long as you remember that your happiness and therefore our happiness as a couple are made up of two individuals, then I believe we will be alright."

Amazing! James or at least my pretend James has it. His message does not constrict or forbid and it allows Sally to feel his commitment and love for her without her feeling choked.

Of course, for every situation and every significant relationship, the needs and tolerances will be different.

If we stay with James and Sally a little longer we can see that their ability to be honest is paramount. The moment that one does not "own the truth," whatever that may be, then the hope we just witnessed crumbles.

If, for instance, James says what he believes Sally needs to hear to keep her happy, or, if Sally doesn't admit that she goes out with her friends to meet men (if that's the case) then the opportunity is lost.

For me, it doesn't matter that James doesn't feel he can give Sally permission to do as she likes, or that Sally might be sleeping with other men.

The only thing that matters is that they broke down when it came to honesty. Tell it like it is for you and see if the response is what you need.

If James needs to put Sally on a leash, she can either be put there happily or resist, but she must know his needs honestly.

If she cannot be tied down then she either negotiates with James for more freedom and a new set of rules for their relationship or she blows it up.

It is exactly the same with James.

If Sally needs the attention of other men and James is ok with that, then they can act like consenting adults and do what they need to.

If, on the other hand, James cannot comply happily with Sally's needs then they re-negotiate to a place they can both live with or they move apart.

I could go on forever. The point, I hope is clear.

If the relationship, any important relationship, has a basis of permission then it stands a wonderful chance for long term survival.

For what it's worth I offer it here in a nutshell. Stick it on the fridge and offer it up as a hopeful, exciting, kind way to live.

"I care for you my friend, my love, and I very much want you to be happy. I give you permission to pursue your happiness and to please take me with you.

I know at times I will get lost or fall behind. I need you to remember that I care for you and your needs.

When I cannot keep up or understand then I will ask you to help me.

When it comes apart I ask you to be patient and, if necessary, negotiate with me so that I too can find peace and happiness in your needs fulfilled.

If I can no longer keep up or understand, if we cannot find "a spot" after communicating, negotiating and being honest, then I will let you go.

I will encourage you to move on to a place that I only wish I could go.

Please remember my weaknesses and my fragility.

Remember that I long to be with you in your change and your growth but that at times I get lost in my own needs and fears.

Please remember, finally, that my happiness is your happiness and that I trust that you will keep both of us in mind as often as you can.

Never, however, let your feelings for me keep you from finding peace and contentment.

We will resist the six ugly words in our friendship or our love relationship.

We will try to be as honest and open as possible. We will remember each other's frailties and weaknesses and we will operate from a place of love and understanding.

I will not should or shouldn't you, tell you you are right or wrong, good or bad. I will simply try and stay close to you.

I will bare my changing, needy, often confused, frightened soul and together we will work to figure it out.

You are important and I care for you.
Be happy my friend, the rest will follow."

To quote Charles (the cancer Doctor) once again "so much of it just doesn't matter." Your honest, communication and permission for me to be myself and find myself is all that matters.

Listen

With permission the possibilities are endless. Nevertheless, there is still the feeling of being lost and unable to navigate. In the end the feeling of needing to return to what is known and sure is almost certain to win out.

Robert and I spoke of this very thing.

"Please understand, I want to do it differently, I want to change and try.
I want to grab hold and do what's necessary for change and growth.
But this permission stuff is foreign to me.
To be perfectly honest I am frightened of the risk and the unknown.
The thought is appealing and the words are lovely, but hey, I really still have no idea what to do or how to do it.
I want more than to put away the TV and read a book and I am not yet able to offer my friends or the "loves" in my life the permission to be free, and live the life they need.
Please, can you help a little more? I like the tune, but have no idea how to dance."

I have urged you to do it differently, and I understand the pull to the past. I understand the power of yesterday. You may not necessarily like life the way you live it, but it is understandable and therefore comfortable.

The words that I declared war on and their power are formidable. Indeed, they are immense in their influence and their ability to capture and control.

They are us.

Most of us have been raised on should and shouldn't, right and wrong and good and bad. They are and have been a kind of mother's milk for our development. Very few of us have been trained differently. We now know that their power runs deep.

The religions that we were raised on offered them up. Our education system held them in place, and our very own families, our parents especially, taught us even in the safe, trusted spot of our homes, to honor and respect them.

Because I know this, have felt their power and influence, and because I live in the same world with the same pressures as you, I offer up the following.

These are a few concrete places where you or you and yours might try, for real, in your daily life to actually begin to escape the hold of the powerful, controlling, life numbing six, and actually try something completely new and different.

Know that this is simply a representation of what I have been going on about. Know that if you can find a way to do and feel even some of these, then the Red Letters have begun to loosen their grasp and you have begun to consider new possibilities.

This list will show opportunity, and will in fact demonstrate real ways to leave yesterday and all it holds behind.

These will allow you to imagine that today might be different. Imagine for real, new ways to act, to be, and to see.

They will allow you something new. Places where you can feel the change, where others experience it and the Red Letters will hate it.

Absolutely first and foremost with no exception that I can conceive of, the primary starting place is for you to listen.

This means a couple of things.

First it means to listen to you carefully. Your insides are eager and keen to try something new. Your insides are happy for different.

I know I have spent hours telling you that the Red Letters control and influence us. True, but beyond the robot, sheep stuff that I have made fun of and warned you against, there is that part of you, that special well guarded, protected part, that cries at movies when no one is looking, that cheers for the underdog or that is fully tired of the routine and the grind.

That part of you is so eager for new and different. Listen to it. It is what Robert brought me at the beginning, when he begged for something new, something that would keep it together and make him feel happy.

If you can manage to find that spark or flame, depending on your ability to risk and try new, if you can locate the person inside, who is touched by joyful emotion and who identifies with the underdog. The one who struggles against the odds, to win or change or figure it out, then you will have found the starting point.

For some people, like Christina, this is enormous and needs no invitation or retraining. For others, however, that spark must be located and nurtured.

Once you have been able to listen for your voice of change, the voice that says,

"Hey, I like the idea of something new.
I want to try.
I want to risk and learn."
Then you are well on your way.

If you are inclined, the rest will follow.

If this all sounds like folly, then you have only wasted a few dollars (on this ridiculous book) and no damage has been done.

The second part of listen is much more difficult. Listening to yourself is one thing, but to listen to others and to what goes on around you is very different and very difficult.

I have heard it said, that we were born with one mouth and two ears and that we are meant to use them proportionately.

That's a hard task. We like to talk, and when we are not talking we are off in our own world figuring out what we are going to say next.

I'm speaking to you and you either go off on something that I said, all on your own not hearing me at all, or you are already in the middle of my story, formulating your response. Your response, may or may not have anything to do with what I was going on about, but what's that got to do with it?

The point is, if you can sit and listen to others, strangers, friends and loved ones, then you will realize how powerful the Red Letters are and you will see places where you might want to change. You will hear, maybe for the first time, how judgmental, "I" centered, insecure, segregating and hateful we can be.

Once you hear it, you might be able to say,
This is not for me. This is silly and ugly. I want and I need something else.

This is the point where you join Raymond, Christina and Robert.

This is the point where the lights go on and you actually find yourself saying, "Oh my God, I need to change; I need to do it differently."

Once you are here, then maybe a lesson or two on keeping quiet with your mouth and your mind, and you are ready for permission and its magic.

First, find it in yourself, somehow to listen both ways, to yourself, and to others, and then have a look at these.

The List

If you have come this far and are still with me, know that we are here. There is pretty much nowhere else to go except (accept) to try it.

Try different, try new possibilities.

Try and realize, actually feel that yesterday's power is truly limited by who and what we want for our tomorrow. There is no need to tell the same story or sing the same song.

"I don't want or need to be that person any more. I get the permission thing. I am excited by it and I am ready to try."

Some of this may sound a little odd, even silly. I ask that you remember that silly may be the price of brand new and certainly the price of completely fresh.

There will be consequences. Some that you know may caution you, judge you, even reject or shun you. They understood the old you and were likely comfortable with it.

The new you may cause them to feel excluded or worse judged, because they have not changed, they have nothing new.

I want you to know, however, that in all of life, in each thing we are involved in everyday, in more ways than we can imagine, there are tradeoffs.

For every choice, every decision and every move there are pluses and minuses.

Stay home from work, instead of showing up, gain a day off, feel guilty.
Buy a sports car instead of a family car. Eat up the attention, include others.
Live in a condo over a house, less maintenance, big condo fee.
Take a trip or pay off a bill. Feel rested, feel relieved.
Marry for love or money, happiness or wealth.
Marry the blond not the brunette. I leave that one with you.

Every choice we make has consequences. Every choice has pluses and minuses. Very seldom, unless there is something clearly horrible, malicious or illegal involved, can we say that the choice was clear and the consequences obvious. For every choice there are definitely pros and cons.

The permissions that most interest me are the ones with important consequences. I mean the ones that affect others as well as you.

First give yourself permission to do it, see it, consider it, and live it differently. This reassessment of you, how you act, how you react and respond will most certainly affect you, but it will also be huge to those around you.

Mommy used to cry every time she got frustrated. Now she sits and says, "I feel frustrated" and she talks about how she feels.

Daddy was always angry. He would yell and scream for what seemed like no reason at all. Now he tells us what makes him upset and more than that he even laughs at himself.

My wife wears nice clothes every day. The clothes that she would only wear on special occasions she wears all the time. She looks beautiful and happy. She told me that every day for her from now on was going to be a special occasion. It's great to be around her. We all feel different. I know she lost a couple of her friends; they made fun of her and said that she thought she was too good for them. She doesn't seem to care. She just does it differently.

Only days ago I had dinner with Sandy. She was thrilled to open a new bottle of wine.

"I just received this bottle as a gift from my brother. He knows a lot about wine. He said it was good. That means it's expensive. Usually I would keep it, you know, save it for God knows when. It would collect dust and I would "never be good enough" or have an occasion "big

enough" to drink it. Look, I already have it opened. I am no longer going to save the best for last."

The list is endless, the benefits endless also.

What, you like what's going on with you and around you so much that change seems ridiculous?

Give yourself permission to say "No."

No I do not agree.
I do not want to do what you are doing.
I will not be a fool or a jerk.
I will not continue to be uncaring and selfish.
I will no longer act like a child.
I will be a better person today than I was yesterday.

Give yourself permission to say "Yes."

Yes I will stop and think.
Yes I want more from my life.
Yes I can be better, be kinder and more caring.
Yes I can do it different.

Give yourself permission to reject.

I will no longer simply be part of a mindless group.
I will not care for and be influenced by gossip.
I will turn off the TV and think on my own.

I will give myself permission to be an individual and not hope to be accepted by the crowd no matter what the cost.

I am a person responsible for my life and I will act accordingly.

Do you remember earlier when I spoke of the power, the awesome power of the popular, smart high school student who stepped out of the group to be interested and decent to a student with a "lesser social status"? This student has enormous power by simply choosing to act with decency, compassion and caring for another. They set a new standard by their actions. All eyes are on them because in their small world they are supremely important.

The examples and teachings of the teachers and administrators are of no large importance, but the actions and words of the popular student are immense. In their world, the world of high school, the popular students set the tone and the pace and they decide what's acceptable and unacceptable. If they choose to say wait or stop or hold on let's do it differently, there will be immediate change. The popular high school student who sits with those less popular at lunch or helps those less able in class controls their world. They have the opinions and the actions of others in their hands.

The rest of the world is not so different. You control a large portion of your world, and you influence those around you.

If you choose to be gentler, kinder, more compassionate and caring, those around you have only two choices.

They can reconsider themselves or they can turn and reject you. Either way you may be the winner.

Say no to stupidity and to robot, sheep-like behavior (I know this is a favorite of mine).

So much of what we do, what we are, and what we have become, is influenced by others. We long to belong and to be included. We seem to need to fit in so much that we have forgotten to think. If it's popular or fashionable we want it and need it.

Many people where I live don't use a turn signal. I can cut a corner, great idea. Look, throwing garbage out the window of the car seems to be the norm. Great, who needs a garbage can? Wow, grey is the new car color. I must have one. Everybody has a phone in their ear. I'll do that too.

Come on, change it up. Be you, think on your own. Reject the popular and pay attention to the things that matter and make a difference. Go ahead, get in the face of should and shouldn't, right and wrong, good and bad. Go ahead, reject the givens, do it different.

So very much of what we do, how we act, how we think, and even what we buy into has nothing whatsoever to do with us, our needs and our core. Rather, it is all about the programmed, and the expected. For many when they think about important changes in the way they live they might stop smoking, put down the glass and live without careless, reckless behaviour. These tradition life changes are positive but still a long way from my point.

Changing how you communicate, how you find the courage to be honest, how you listen to others, is the point. Working on not judging and how you relate to the world around you as a caring responsible person who says, "No thanks, I don't want it that way anymore," is what responsible, hopeful, development is all about.

All this is in response to the dreaded words.

It's all a reaction to the "shoulds and shouldn'ts, rights and wrongs, goods and bads" in our life and our world. Somebody decided and told somebody else and somebody else and so on and so on and before you know it, the whole neighborhood or community, country or world is following something written for a very specific reason hundreds or thousands of years ago.

Or worse, somebody heard something on the radio or the "whatever show" and now if you don't follow the suggestion of the day, you are wrong or damned or unpopular or….

I ask you to consider the unusual. God knows the usual, the norm and the expected, never led to anything but mediocrity and "oh well maybe we had better try again."

You might consider this a good time to dig deep and draw on your courage. Courage to say no, or wait, or yes, or not me, or I want to do it differently.

This is the power of the Red Letters. They control us, force us into camps and have us living our entire lives based on the power of tradition, or worse, the power of the group.

Gandhi wrote "We must be the change that we want to see in the world."

We have been brought to our spot in life by the will and force of the words I have warned you about.

I am a good person because I live up to the expectations of others.
I will surely get into heaven because I have followed all the rules.
My parents are proud of me because I understand exactly what to do in all situations.
I am a model person. I have it all figured out.

Or maybe this.

I will no longer be unhappy, and directed by forces that couldn't care less about me.
I will remember Gandhi's words and be the change I require and the world needs.
I will give a damn and I will care for myself in new and different ways.
I will do it different.
I will wear my best clothes every day.

Tomorrow

I have long believed that many people seek to do things differently. I am certain that there are a great number who would like a change, a new approach and an alternative.

I am equally sure that so many who seek change are not exactly sure what they seek to change from.

This look into our systems and ourselves provides some possibilities.

For me, the Red Letters, should and shouldn't, right and wrong and good and bad are the key to our struggle, our "control" and our unhappiness. Sometimes it simply helps to name things. Once we know what we fight or struggle against, then we have a much better idea how to succeed.

The Red Letters control, separate, judge, manipulate and limit who and what we are. They stilt our growth and they determine how we are going to act and re-act long before the situation arises.

This is exactly what has been and continues to be intended. We are not meant to be completely miserable, neither are we to be happy.

The forces that dictate who and what we are, and how we choose to be, have worked very hard through penetrating all places that we can imagine with segregation, separation and small mindedness. Some clues have been offered and maybe more importantly, some real ways to combat, confront and even defeat the power of the nasty words.

I know that people do things when they are ready. That just because I am ready for things to change does not mean that change is imminent. You have here a few observations, descriptions and possibilities that might bring you opportunity to live differently and take some risks.

I am certain that the power of the six words is not easily overturned or even ignored. They are formidable and have spent centuries gaining hold and developing roots, and their greatest ally is not the education system, the religious system or our parents. No, the greatest support of the horrid words and their power is us.

You and I, we are their champions. We are the ones who participate in the daily ugliness, judgment, small minded-ness and horrible debilitating behavior towards our fellow person that truly give the Red Letters the smug, never ending power that they seem to have.

We are the bearers of the pain and hatred, and we are the only ones who can stop the unnecessary pounding on our neighbor, our self and our humanity.

Many among us will never surrender the weapon they have against the other or the human race. Many among us thrive on the debilitating power of being able to scold, judge, divide and punish. Many we know do not wish to change a thing. They enjoy the hurt and the control. They thrive on us and them. They have no desire for betterment, hope, communication and honesty. They are small and seek small. They will never reform.

The Red Letters are their friends.

The ugly history of human kind tends too often to be blamed on a few. It is the leaders among us who whip up the unsuspecting masses to think and do horrible things. If only we could rid the world of the terrible power mongers among us, we would see the improvement immediately.

Nonsense! We are too easily let off the hook and we are too often excused of our responsibility.

We are the villains, too often too eager to participate in the downfall of others. Too often too quick to judge, divide, ridicule and separate.

Our problems are ours. Our hatred and pettiness belong to us and our institutions are able to be changed instantly by those who control them, us. If I am correct, and there are a huge number, maybe even the majority who, like Robert, Christina and me are tired of the limitation, the conformity and the control of unhappiness, then remember your ability to fight mediocrity, viscous circles and misery.

Pay attention to your need to relate. Question places that have pat, certain answers. Look for alternatives to how we relate and communicate and do not forget that you have the ability to provide permission to yourself and to others.

The power of permission is your best weapon. It will allow you to say, wait or stop or yes or no. It will allow you to re-examine and reconsider. It will allow you to see it all and even live it all differently.

I want to pay attention.

I want to do what makes me happy.

I like the idea of those around me happy.

I will not go through life angry or miserable or sad or told. I will listen to myself, my needs and my wants.

I will care for others and I will try to do it different and better in the name of hope, change and new every day.

Give permission freely.
Give it to grow and experiment.
Give it to make mistakes and risk.
Mostly, give it to be human.
Give it, with our faults and weaknesses,
our blemishes and our frailties.
Give it with understanding and compassion.
Give it as you would want it to be given, with hope
and help for a better tomorrow and a better,
different you.

Remember that permission begets permission. If you could meet and see Christina, my poster child for permission and possibility, she would make you smile and want to do it different. She would make the coldest heart melt and desire things never imagined.

You have heard the saying "dance like no one is watching."

I suggest that you "live like everyone is watching all the time."

Just like Christina, with unbridled enthusiasm and magnificent hope that anything is possible and no change is too great to make.

Try telling people what you need and while you're at it, try giving them some of that in return. Permission inspires. It frees absolutely and it is nothing but hope for something new and different.

Permission is not concerned with details or things of little importance. Charles (the cancer doctor) taught me that so much doesn't matter.

So much is wasted and worn out on the things that only weigh us down, wear us down and make us succumb again to the ominous six.

Permission will allow you to ask the really important questions. Who am I and what do I want out of life? How can I be a better, more loving, tolerant, decent, considerate person, while allowing, and encouraging others, with my permission, to do the same?

Your acceptance of me makes all the difference.

Of course we need to constantly re-evaluate and reconsider who we are and what we want.

How can I grow here?
How do I respond kinder and gentler?
How do I make a positive difference?

The world is full of pain and problems. We search for common answers and find only division. For every issue there are a million experts with ten thousand expert opinions.

Remember how your blue seems yellow to another.
How steadfast rules here, are silly there and how truths are exchanged as borders are crossed.

Doing it differently, peeling off the old requires courage and a conviction to risk. This is very difficult. "The letters" and their allies are intolerant of change. They loath adjustment and alteration and they have no patience for humanity.

By putting on the power of change you put on a suit never tried on. It brings you to the candy store with choice and the amusement park with wonder. The ways are many, the consequences great and the freedom immense. You truly hold your life and its happiness in your hands. More importantly you hold the happiness of others and the very future of the world.

Take permission to not be yesterday's person anymore. They are aimless, trapped, or simply lost.

There is no benefit to continuing to be a solider of should and shouldn't, right and wrong and good and bad. They require your submission, your small mindedness, your hatred towards others and your very happiness.

Celebrate your imperfections. Enjoy your humanity. We are sad and weak, vulnerable and ridiculously flawed.

No we are not meant to give up and feel beaten. We are simply to acknowledge who and what we are, what we need and proceed with hope and forgiveness for our self and our neighbors.

I do not do it all right. I am weak, sad and lost and I love trying to figure it out and do it different and better today than I did yesterday.

Ask what you need for life, seek it with wonder, hope and permission, feeling enthusiastic about the trip and give that same thing to those you encounter.

You must know that your acceptance, encouragement and permission to be me and to figure, fall and explore mean everything to me.

Let the manipulation and restraining, unnecessary rules give way to, I will try to understand, to encourage and to accept.

I will be as forgiving of your fragility, weakness and humanity as I can.

Please be as kind to me.

Perspective

The work before you was written out of observations and experiences made over a lifetime. There is no intention here to win you over to change of any kind. This work is selling nothing. Rather, the sole purpose of ***Under Pressure*** is thought, reflection and conversation. If after reading this little book you feel able to consider things differently or even talk about the contents as food for thought, then I have succeeded in my desire to have us look at ourselves and the world around us. I have been told that ***Under Pressure*** can shake our foundation and leave us questioning many things that may have previously been taken for granted or intentionally "left alone".

Know that the purpose of these words is not to have you abandon the things you hold dear but rather simply to understand them, their motivation and limitations. In order to balance the concern that some have expressed over the "controversy" and "power" of ***Under Pressure*** I offer you balance. When the words were first complete I circulated them to a few people I knew well and to a few who were at arm's length. The following comments are representatives of what came back to me from the early readers.

First Testimonials

"There are so few times that I am moved to tears. The words in "Relationships" had the tears rolling down my face. WOW, Powerful. I actually didn't think that men were capable of that level of sensitivity and for j to put his thoughts and insights so powerfully and with such compassion on paper leaves me in awe. These words will not leave me any time soon."

Lee, Elementary School Teacher

"I can't think of a single area of my life that isn't different since I read the book. I sit up straighter, I take more pleasure in work and my family, I enjoy doing the laundry, and I'm kinder to clients. Little things and big things- all different now. I drink less (alcohol), eat more fruit and vegetables. I think happier thoughts, I parent more calmly.

Marlene, Investment Banker

Further testimonials at www.changeitbooks.com

John Martin has lived an interesting life. Adopted as an infant, he spent much of his early life in a military family, lost and lonely, finding it difficult to establish roots or connections. The family moved numerous times from military posting to military posting.

Educated in Philosophy and Theology at university John was ordained a Protestant minister, serving in that capacity for ten years. During his time as a cleric, John became interested in specialized ministry. He worked on the streets of Toronto with the homeless, needy, disenfranchised and lost. From there, he spent the next several years as chaplain in the cancer ward of a large Canadian hospital.

While working in hospital John became involved in caring for the dying and the grieving. He has extensive experience in bereavement counseling for individuals and groups and has lectured and taught grief support, communication skills and ethics to physicians, health care professionals and volunteer groups. John spent considerable time not only in the assistance of those hurting over the loss of a loved one, but he also became involved in the lives of many who struggled with their illness, the meaning of their life and often their eventual death. John

Martin has had the unique opportunity to see life from places few will ever see.

He has spent years with those who are desperate and in crisis and understands hurt and broken from his own life. He uses his years of experience and his own life struggles to help us understand that there are so many possibilities unknown and unexplored that can truly have us living differently and understanding and appreciating our lives and all around us from a new and hopeful point of view.

John is among the few men who can claim to be the primary care giver of a child. He and his wife have a son who is now 17 and while she works long hours as a physician, John is the one who has and continues to stay home.

J. Martin is the author of *I Can't Stop Crying...Grief and Recovery a Compassionate Guide* and *One Left of L...How to Get Along With Others.* He is also a contributor to *I Don't Know What to Say...How to Help and Support Someone Who is Dying* by Dr. Robert Buckman.